VISIBILISING WOMEN

Facets of History Through a Gender Lens

VISIBILISING WOMEN

Facets of History Through a Gender Lens

Kirit K. Shah
Radhika Seshan

Publications

KALPAZ PUBLICATIONS
DELHI-110 052

Visibilising Women: Facets of History Through a Gender Lens

Rs. 690

ISBN : 81-7835-415-2

Published in 2005 in India by
Kalpaz Publications,
C-30, Satyawati Nagar,
Delhi-110 052
Email : kalpaz@hotmail.com

Lasertype Setting by: Tact Computer Graphics, Delhi
Printed at: Salasar Imaging System, Delhi

Contents

Acknowledgements

Antiquity tends to automatically confer a certain distinction, and India, as one of the oldest civilizations in the world, undoubtedly has many distinctive features. However, antiquity need not confer sanctity. There are many features visible in society today, which are none too savoury, and it is here that the study of history becomes relevant, for it helps us to understand the ways in which society has been shaped, and the reasons for that shaping. Women in Indian society, as everywhere, constitute half of its members, and yet, figure very little in its historiography. The papers collected here are an attempt in that direction, through a feminist lens.

This anthology has originated out of papers presented at a number of seminars organized by the Department of History, SNDT Women's University, Mumbai. The Department has, as a general rule, organized at least one seminar every year, and has also organized one National Seminar. The theme of the National Seminar was gender, but most of the papers presented were on women. This clearly reflects that 'gender' as a category of historical analysis is taken to be synonymous with woman/women only. Seven papers of this collection were presented at our National Seminar, while six come from three other seminars held earlier. The paper of Usha Thakkar is actually the script of the Second Sau. Shanta Gambhir Memorial Lecture delivered by her last year. We feel deeply beholden to her.

The papers collected in this volume are of uneven quality. By and large, the original scripts have been retained, though in a few cases, extensive re-writing was necessary. Whatever changes have been made, were deemed important, taking into account the comments made during the discussions at the various seminars at which these papers were presented. Changes have also been made at certain places to make the language more lucid and readable. The editors are aware that some papers are incomplete by way of references, but we regret to have to say that the authors did not provide the references, despite reminders.

No diacritical marks have been used in the text. We believe that most of the words are familiar enough, and the use of diacritical marks would distract the reader. However, all such words have been italicised. On the whole, the rules laid down by the Indian History Congress for italics, notes and references have been followed.

Our heartfelt thanks to all those who have helped us in putting together this volume, and our apologies to the authors, who have waited patiently for such a long time for their papers to be published. In particular, we must thank the University, for providing financial assistance for all the seminars, and all the delegates for presenting papers, even if we have not included them for publication. Ms. Jaswandi Wamburkar and Ms. Meherjyoti Sangle, faculty members of the Department of History, SNDT University, and Ms. Mrinal Joshi, a Research Scholar of the same department, are thanked here not only for contributing their respective papers, but also working hard to make each of our Seminars a success. Last, but in no way the least, we thank the office staff of the Department of PGSR, Churchgate Campus – Raju, Manoj, Archana, Jeetu – for offering unstinted support in organizing events, and our respective families, for bearing with us while this volume was in the making. Mr. M.B. Deshpande, our typist, is also thanked here for all the hard work involved in preparing the typescript.

List of Contributors

Kamal Abhyankar, former Head, University Department of Sanskrit, SNDT Women's University, Mumbai.

Ramala Buxamusa, former lecturer, RCWS, SNDT Women's University, Mumbai.

Neera Desai, former Director, RCWS, SNDT Women's University, Mumbai.

Soonu Dhanjisha, Head, History Department, SNDT College of Arts, Churchgate, Mumbai.

Manisha Dikholkar, former Head, History Department, Elphinstone College, Mumbai.

Mrinal Joshi, Research Scholar, University Department of History, SNDT Women's University, Mumbai.

Makrand Mehta, Emeritus Professor of History, Gujarat University, Ahmedabad, and University Professor, University of Sutherland, UK.

Shirin Mehta, former Head, Department of History, Gujarat University, Ahmedabad.

Archana Mishra, Research Scholar, University Department of History, SNDT Women's University, Mumbai.

Ranjana Mishra, Head, History Department, M.D. Shah Mahila College, Mumbai.

Padmaja Patil, Reader, Department of History, Shivaji University, Kolhapur.

Purabi Ghosh Roy, Reader in History, Maharshi Dayanand College, Mumbai.

Meherjyoti Sangle, Lecturer, Department of PGSR in History, SNDT Women's University, Mumbai.

Radhika Seshan, Lecturer, Department of History, University of Pune, Pune.

Kirit K. Shah, Professor and Head, University Department of History, SNDT Women's University, Mumbai.

Kunjalata Shah, Former Head, Department of History, SNDT College of Arts, Mumbai.

Usha Thakkar, Hon. Director, Institute of Research on Gandhian Thought and Rural Development, Mani Bhavan Gandhi Sangrahalaya, Mumbai.

Jaswandi Wamburkar Utagikar, Lecturer, University Department of History, SNDT Women's University, Mumbai.

Sushma J. Varma, Professor, Department of History, University of Pune, Pune.

Introduction

K.K. Shah and Radhika Seshan

The collection of papers put together here has grown out of several seminars organized by the University Department of History, SNDT Women's University, Mumbai, with a view to motivating and encouraging researchers to re-read and re-interpret the conventional sources of history and locate voices of women or collect references to female experiences in the past. In either case, the expected gain was to visibilise women in a variety of historical contexts. The starting point in planning the exercise was the feminist rejection of available historiography, that documented the experience of only one half of the human race, glossing over facts of female experience incidentally accommodated in the conventional sources of history. It will be seen that this modest collection consists primarily of micro-studies, each aiming to capture an aspect of complex social reality of a civilization of sub-continental dimension. The common thread running through the papers is the feminist perspective of the past, pleading a place for women in its accepted and official version, so as to impart completeness to the picture to the extent possible. If anything, the collection brings home the point that a lot can be recovered in the field even with conventional tools and methods applied to conventional sources of history.

Within the theoretical framework provided by the feminist understanding, there have, in recent years, been a large number of studies on various aspects of Indian history, which make rigorous attempts to read between the lines of the sources, and to explore alternative sources for the study of the past. This has resulted in a wealth of material being made available to the student of history. The first paper in this compendium, that of Neera Desai, is an attempt to place the study of women in the context of such new writings on history. Beginning with a brief analysis of the earlier writings on women, especially that of A.S. Altekar, she goes on to analyse the nature of the change that has occurred, and identifies three major areas in which a change is visible. The first change is in the rewriting of political history, where women's participation in the national movement, in particular, is highlighted. A continuation of this approach makes gender difference a key to the analysis of social realities. The next major change that she identifies is that of looking at woman as an agency, in which she highlights the importance of oral history.

Carrying on with the idea of agency is the paper of Soonu Dhanjisha, which examines agency through the lens of religion, and more importantly, what she terms 'feminist theology'. This, she defines as 'theology seen through the experience of being a woman in a man's world'. The paper examines the nature of the prescriptive roles laid out for women, and the social application of such roles. It is not an empirical piece of research, but an attempt at explicating androcentric evolution of various theologies. Thus, it is not feminist theology as such, as might be the impression from the title, but theology through a feminist lens, with a historical perspective. Dhanjisha argues that one can trace the parallel developments in society through an analysis of the various norms and standards laid out for women through history.

Among the prescriptive texts of Ancient India, the *Smrti* of Manu occupies a central place, being the most comprehensive in its content and authoritative in the area it commands. Its injunctions elevating women to honourable place in the family and society have often been quoted and cited to show the high status accorded to women in the ancient past. However, with the birth of subaltern consciousness in the colonial past, it was attacked and even rejected as a source of law, being based on invidious distinctions between man and man and advocating unquestioned dominance of the Brahmanical elite. With the spread of feminism in academia and its project of rewriting history, the anti-feminist content of the text came into focus, inviting severe condemnation in the process, so much so that even mention of Manu has become taboo, as being a misogynist of the first order. Against this background, the paper of Archana Mishra is a bold attempt to explain the contradictory content of the text on women, arguing that it is necessary to eschew generalizations on either side, in view of the fact that the available text is not homogeneous. On the contrary, it evolved over a period of at least four centuries, and contains layers and layers of diverse origins in terms of time and space, making it extremely problematic for the final compiler to iron out the glaring inconsistencies and discrepancies entering into the ideals and injunctions about women. The paper closes with a plea to view the text in the totality of the situation in which it originated and evolved.

Few women of Ancient India have found a place in history for their scholarship, and names casually coming to mind are those figuring in Vedic literature. There is near unanimity on the opinion that formal education was denied to women and those belonging to royal and aristocratic circles were given specific kind of education, generally confined to the fine arts. In this context the small paper of Kamal Abhyankar on Avantisundari is a welcome attempt to put together scattered references that prove that this *Kshatriya-Kanya,* married to Brahman Rajasekhara, was a learned lady harbouring deep love for Prakrit language and literature. If anything, the paper shows that a good many Avantisundaris are waiting to be discovered in the vast corpus of ancient literature, who must have made contributions of no mean merit, though they lived and worked within the known framework of Brahmanical patriarchy.

Studies on Brahmanical patriarchy are many, but it must be remembered that this is not the only kind of patriarchy visible in India. Here, the paper of Ramala Baxamusa makes a valuable addition in attempting to understand the nature of problems faced by Muslim women, through a study of Islamic law. Pre-Islamic laws denied women almost all rights, for women were regarded as a commodity. Female infanticide was apparently common. The coming of Islam did change a number of things, for, among other things, the Prophet opposed female infanticide, and granted women rights over any property that she inherited or earned. However, after the Prophet's death, and with the coming of the four major schools of jurisprudence, women's position once again suffered; and between then and now, women's position in accepted Islamic law has continued to decline. In India, she points out that even post-independence, there has not been much improvement in the position of women, for though the ulema were 'aware that the existing Islamic laws were going against the true Islamic practices', they were not making any effort to bring about a change, in tune with the ideals of the Prophet as well as the requirements of the modern world.

The history of medieval India, especially as regards women, is an area where considerable research needs to be done. Here, the paper of Mrinal Joshi is an important contribution. Among the cruelest of Indian customs based on gender bias, that of burning a widow on the funeral pyre of her husband has been debated the most down the ages. The earliest recorded testimony of its antiquity comes from Greek accounts. They conclude, after graphically narrating the event, "some of the Greeks present reprobated such rites as barbarous and cruel." The latest of its occurrences should have come from the year 1829 when the Governor-General in Council passed Regulation XVII on Dec. 4th to the effect, "A Regulation for declaring the practice of suttee or of burning or burying alive the widows of Hindoos, illegal and punishable by the criminal courts." Sporadic incidents in evidence of the continued hold of the custom have consistently occurred till the close of the 20th century. Charanshah, the wife of Manshah, flung herself on the funeral pyre of her husband on Nov. 11, 1999. The ironic reality of her act reflected in the contradictory attitude of the villagers of Satpura (Dist. Mahoba, U.P.) is beautifully brought out by Subhash Mishra in his report, a passage from which is well worth citing. "The poor Dalit woman, who single-handedly looked after her ailing husband–

the villagers refused to accompany her to the cremation ground because he had TB – has suddenly become an object of worship. She is the Satimata, a new icon in the region. Shunned when alive, she has nearly acquired the status of a goddess now." (Subhash Mishra, "Medieval Madness", *India Today*, November 29, 1999, p. 59). This single example of the callous, cruel and contradictory attitude of society towards the supreme self-sacrifice of a woman communicates much more on the nature and operation of the custom in the name of time-honoured tradition than a bulky volume on its history, for this is not even a case of society seeking legitimation from the past after inventing a tradition.

At the height of Roop Kanwar's self-immolation controversy in the late eighties of the last century, Romila Thapar did an exhaustive study of the history and sociology of the custom. She pointed out, "Sati stones like hero stones occur more often, not in fertile agricultural mainlands but in ecologically marginal areas, where local conflicts and skirmishes would be frequent. Possibly in marginal areas, the process of transition from tribe to *jati* may have required an underlining of the new norms which would have implications for the inheritance and status of women." This view of Thapar seems to find strong support in the paper of Mrinal Joshi, who has given a regional and religious break-up of 20 records on sati stones that she has studied. Significantly, 16 inscriptions come from the ecologically marginal regions like Kachch and Saurashtra and in terms of caste affiliations, 11 belong to the warrior class of Rajputs. However, it has to be remembered that hers is a random selection from the records available. Among other interesting facts, she brings out the solitary reference to a husband becoming *sat* after the death of his wife, committing self-immolation as a protest against injustice and the ritual of *kamala-puja*, a form of religious suicide.

For the history of modern India, journalism is a rich source of references on a variety of themes, and with women constituting the core item on the agenda of social reform movements in the colonial past, the wealth of information it contains can hardly be overestimated. Our collection here contains two papers based on examination of the source in Gujarati, locating landmarks in the history of women's consciousness and its articulation in the field of journalism.

The paper of Shirin Mehta investigates women's consciousness through popular writings, literature and journalism of the period 1850-1920 in Gujarat. The article raises fundamental questions such as differentiating women's perception of contemporary issues from those of men; viewing women's issues in terms of ethnic diversity, class character and gender category, sensing the tone of ideology they focused upon or the type of clientele they commanded. She has divided the development of women's consciousness into three phases, starting with Eurocentric writing in the mid-19th century and ending with the opening decades of the 20th century, when women's writings acquired subjectivity and centrality.

The paper of Kunjlata Shah is based on her study of the popular Gujarati journal for women, *Sundari Subodh*, and brings out women's voices registered in its writings during the period 1903-1923. The central concern of the paper is to probe the extent to which the hegemonic patriarchal ideology of the cultural revivalists shaped women's perceptions about themselves.

The paper of Makrand Mehta, also dealing with women of Gujarat shows that there are hardly any systematic attempts at tracing accounts of women's grassroots organizations of the pre-Gandhian era. The author argues that perceptions and methods of its organizers differed from those of western educated intelligentsia, who operated at the abstract level of struggle, that hardly helped widows in their cheerless existence. The paper explicates this point with a case study of the *Vanita Vishram*, Surat, that was founded by Bajigouri Munshi and Shivgauri alias Naniben Gajjar, who happened to be child widows. This institution-building exercise in a way represented the process of translating the reform agenda at the ideological level into a concrete action plan at grassroots level. The paper covers the period 1907-1920, documenting the innovative efforts of women at self-help.

If the concept of a revolution in history represents a fundamental change in the life of a society, it is invariably preceded by the birth and growth of new ideas and goals and the intellectuals who conceive them could truly be called architects of such a revolution. Such thinkers and philosophers, though products of their own times, necessarily transcend it, so as to shape the nature and chart the course of the revolution they visualize. The so-called Renaissance in 19th century India was in essence a comprehensive plan and programme of socio-religious reform, conceived on the twin bases of caste abolition and upliftment of the condition of women, so as to usher in universal human values. The task before the intellectual leaders of this Renaissance was verily challenging, in terms of offering a convincing critique of contemporary Hindu society, and forcefully arguing for change without walking out of it. Painful indeed must have been this waging of war, in which attacking the tradition, and yet belonging to it, amounted to continuous tearing of one's conscience. Gopal Hari Deshmukh, better known as Lokahitawadi, was one such thinker, who lived, life-long, the trauma of a troubled conscience. Yet another challenge confronting intellectuals like him was to offer a complete and comprehensive programme touching every aspect of the contemporary society, which needed extensive study and perceptive understanding of the issues involved. Encyclopaedic indeed was the range of articles and books authored by him, and it is not possible to bracket him under any ideological label. So representative was he of his times that he has truly been called the 'living history of Maharashtra of those times'. It has now become necessary to locate and organize the material encompassing his views on a given item of reform agenda, for some of the items that he talked or wrote about have developed into independent movements. Usha Thakkar in her paper has undertaken this taxing task, not only to compile his views on women's conditions, but to contextualise them in the totality of the discourse in which he was participating. It should be remembered that, given that a substantial corpus of his writings are in Marathi, her article opens up the source material to a wider circle of researchers.

Reference has been made above to the institution of sati, the burning of widows in the name of time-honoured custom. Equally barbaric is the custom of female infanticide, which is something that still flourishes, albeit in a clandestine manner. The phenomenon of killing the girl child is no longer of academic interest or an area of historical research alone, for its continued manifestation, even after several stringent legal measures and the spread of education in our own generation, makes it a matter of national shame and calls for multi-disciplinary research. One does not have to go very far to locate the continuance of this cruel practice and its widespread character across various castes and communities in the new millennium. The census data bring home the bias against accepting and rearing the girl child. The editorial of the Mumbai edition of *The Times of India* dated 14 September 2004 comments on the details of the last census, "The census figures showing that the sex ratio is more skewed in cities than in rural areas shatters the myth that an urban mind-set is necessarily more evolved. It shows that literacy and better health care facilities do not foster gender equality. In fact, technology has become a means with which to eliminate the girl child." Obviously, the bias appears to be rooted in psyche much more than in any of the social, economic or cultural factors, individually or collectively. Given the complex nature of this cruel practice that has survived all the onslaughts from the forces and processes of modernization, one might wonder what purpose the paper of Purabi Ghosh Roy, a micro study covering a single community that inhabits just a corner of the Indian subcontinent would serve. One hardly needs to point out that even if one views the problem in purely psychological terms, its continuance in the face of modernity could be construed as a hangover from the past. Roy is not oblivious to the psychological dimension of the evil, in which bias pervaded the women's mindset as well. In concluding her analysis, she proceeds from the particular to the general, and says, "The maternal neglect among the Jadejas is a weird expression of women's hostility towards womanhood and also symbolically, towards her own self. This classic instance of the psychological defense of turning against self by identifying with the aggressive male draws attention to the way in which some social institutions have made herself a participant in her self-repudiation and intra-aggression."

Education is undoubtedly of supreme importance in such efforts at self-help and self-reliance. In this context, the paper of Padmaja Patil makes a valuable contribution in identifying the kind of education that was being sought in colonial times. Focusing on Jain women, especially Godubai Upadhye, she points out that, on the whole, the pace of promotion of female education in the Jain community was rather slow. Godubai pointed out that Jain women's education was neglected because the value of education was not very obvious even to the menfolk. The paper makes it clear that, though Godubai was aware of the importance of education, her historical time made her awareness rather limited, for, while she reflected the 19th century awareness of the importance of education she also reflected that century's, and that region's, growing communalization.

One aspect of education that is only now attracting attention is the issue of healthcare. While health itself is primary, studies tracing the development of the mentality and its application are only just beginning. Women have been the 'silent voices of history', who have been 'excluded both as actors and as authors from featuring in history'. In fact, "the exercise of rewriting the past has been confined to invisibilising women: their presence has only been negatively registered, mainly through a vast silence." This observation of Uma Chakravarti and Kumkum Roy ("In Search of our Past", *Economic and Political Weekly*, April 30, 1988) was then largely true. However, the last decades of the last century have seen voluminous literature on women in history from traditional as well as feminist schools of historiography. Whereas the paradigm of history has undergone very little change for researchers in conventional Indian history, in which women still figure in familial frameworks, the feminist researchers have explored many fresh areas. One such area even in mainstream historiography is health and medicine. Women being directly involved in reproduction, the history of their healthcare assumes over-riding importance. The paper of Meherjyoti Sangle focuses on this dark field, and is in the nature of a survey of available historiography. Given the limitations of space, it could not be exhaustive, but it nevertheless covers the contents of numerous works concerning women's history, in which the issue of women's healthcare has been altogether ignored or has been only marginally touched upon. Her paper is thus a valuable contribution in terms of identifying areas of research.

Another potentially rich field of research is that of literature. While much lip-service has been done to the importance of novels and poetry as sources for history, not much work has actually been done, to try to locate a piece of fiction in its own space and time, and therefore to study it in a historical context. Here, the paper of Sushma Varma makes a valuable addition, for it studies not just a novel, Tagore's *Ghare Baire*, but also the film version of the novel. Pointing out that the novel was written at the time of the Swadeshi movement, she tries to show how the novel reflects the growth of the consciousness of Swadeshi among the upper middle classes of Bengal. Tagore's work is a study of the spread of consciousness, and the film based on the book is an example of the continued hold, not just of powerful literature, but also of the ideas that emerged at the time, and still shape our lives.

The next paper picks up one of the ideas outlined in Neera Desai's paper, that of political participation. Examining the nature of gender relations in the Indian National Army, Manisha Dikholkar points out that the role of women was extremely important. Members of the Rani Jhansi Regiment were trained in the use of weapons, and were expected to fight on the battlefield beside men. The INA was thus a visible example of equal participation in the public sphere, in the service of the nation. As she says, women 'did not reject their domestic role but used it as a base to give them strength and legitimacy in their demands'.

While Dikholkar's paper is about the general participation of women in the national movement, Ranjana Mishra focuses on participation of women from the northeastern states in the national movement. Methodologically also, it is different from the others, in that it is based on interviews with survivors, and thus is an exercise in oral history. Many of those who were interviewed carried on with social service in the Gandhian tradition even after independence, for they believed that political independence was only one aspect of what needed to be achieved. However, they faced many problems in their attempts, for, in many cases, they were prevented either from taking up public office itself, or were obstructed in their work if they did manage to get elected to some post. She also points out that, in most cases, if they did get elected, it was to local levels, not the national level. The paper is thus a commentary on the state of affairs after independence, as those who fought for independence were prevented from working for the nation they had helped create.

With the fast development and vast corpus of regional historiography in post-colonial India, it is rightly recognized that most generalizations in mainstream Indian history need to be corrected or qualified, in the light of the radically different picture reflected in regional sources. It is often overlooked that researchers working on the vast canvas of colonial pan-Indian history normally collect their data from contemporary sources in English, with a sprinkling of a few references from regional media, favouring their thesis in a given field of their research. Sources in regional language reflect and represent the experience and perception of the people concerned, and should be treated as more authentic and authoritative than the one available from official English records. This is more so in the context of women's history, when women of a given period and province recorded their views and experiences in their own languages. The paper of Jaswandi Wamburkar Utagikar makes a modest contribution in this regard, based, as it is, on a series of articles authored mostly by women and published in contemporary periodicals. Terming the 20th century as a period of sexual revolution in the West, and locating the impact of European sexual theorists on the Maharashtrian writings, rather than Western Indian, she attempts to explicate the birth of the 'New Woman' and the concept of a 'New Morality', the common basis of both being the premise, "A woman could not be truly liberated till she achieved sexual liberation."

This collection of papers is an exercise not just in documenting various aspects of women's existence, but also in trying to identify areas in which there are large gaps in our knowledge. While education may emphasise rationalism, it is obvious that, in many instances, belief in rationalism is often mere lip service. Religion and religious beliefs continue to shape our lives, and unfortunately, often involves a blind adherence to a historically constructed social reality in the name of religion. It is here that women are often the upholders of the patriarchal traditions. We hope that studies such as this will help in understanding the nature of patriarchal domination and dissemination, for unless we study the nature of historical domination, we cannot challenge that domination.

1

Studying Women in Contemporary India in the Context of New Writings of History

Prof. Neera Desai

Before I discuss the issue of looking at women in contemporary India, a brief glance at new approaches to historiography will not be out of place. For a long time the discussion on position of women began with Prof. A.S. Altekar's renowned work, "*The Position of Women in Hindu Civilization*" and in fact ended with the same book. Not that there were not many books describing the position of women in India, but the approach was more or less the same. Narration was based on "Golden Age" of the Vedic period followed by descriptions of deterioration of the status of women after the second century A.D.

The linear approach of historiography has been posing various problems. The new approach to historical writing resulted from two or three developments. The perception of the past, interpreting the events and their depictions have all been affected in the last few decades. History is no longer just a chronicle of events or a record of ruling dynasties, but also of ordinary men and women. In fact, the social history approach where information on common people, the structure of society at a particular phase in history, family structure, role of religion, nature of economy and such social elements have acquired great significance. A still deeper change came when historians began to look at not merely the lives and achievements of the ruling class but began examining the historical events from below, from the perspective and role of the poor and oppressed people—the so-called subaltern approach, which surely brought about a significant transformation in the ways of looking at historical events and people. However, an even more significant change has been through the method of looking at historical or contemporary events from gender perspective. In the feminist reconstruction of knowledge, the first step was to make women visible in history. As mentioned by Linda Gordon, "We had first to render the invisible visible, the silent noisy, the motionless active." (*Feminist Studies*, p. 21) Thus efforts were made to locate women in various pursuits. In this process, as Gerda Lerner mentions, it was discovered, "Women have a history; women are in history." The search has led among other things to the discovery of the contribution of medieval saints in raising some fundamental questions of patriarchal control over sexuality. Further this has also led to articulation of women-not from the ruling groups - in poetry, referring to their identity, their perception of issues. This has led to rewriting of political history, of women's participation in political transformation, as highlighted in the work. "That Magic Time: Women in the Telangana People's Struggle". The participation of women in mass movements, hints about the feudal-patriarchal attitude in the Communist Party, relegating women to a secondary place, the emotional and subjective experiences of women, all call for fresh perspectives in history writing. (*Recasting Women*, p. 197). The nature of this analysis is not merely additive but substantially transforms the understanding of the role of women in struggles. Scoot while summarizing the 'her-story' approach says that "it has been asserting that personal, subjective experience matters as much as public and political attitudes." (Scoot, p. 20)

This approach, making gender difference a key to the analysis of social relations and public participation, has resulted in scholars looking at the writings of Pandita Ramabai,

Laxmibai Tilak as critiques of patriarchal system, of caste-class differences and not considering women as a homogeneous category.

Yet another approach looks at women as an agency. In spite of the prevalence of patriarchy and encouraging women to be silent sufferers, as revealed in some of the autobiographical writings and in oral history narrations, women have vocalized their sufferings or charted out paths to live life as they wished to live (see Karlekar, Sarkar, Thakkar, Desai). Historians while studying the colonial impact and also examining the emergence of nationalism in the nineteenth century, have been looking at the social reformers and their raising of the women's question.

In short methodological as well as substantial changes have gone into historiography, which has seriously affected the approach of studying women across ages.

Women in Contemporary India

Traditional historians tried to study women in contemporary India as women in economy, polity, education, family etc. With the attainment of Independence and establishment of equality in the Constitution, the mainstream writers were very optimistic about the position of women in Independent India. Women had become 'visible' in education, at work places, in political power positions and in cultural fields. The presence of a woman prime minister sealed all misgivings about the position of women in society.

However the reality was not so bright. The benefits of the post-independence era did not percolate to women of all castes and classes. How did this real situation come to light?

In 1972 the Government of India appointed a Committee to examine the conditions of women at the request of United Nations. After examining the various documents, meeting women leaders in various parts of the country and also touring around the country to personally view the situation, the Committee published its report in 1974 December, entitled "*Towards Equality*". The findings of the Committee were shocking, shattering the complacency of the ruling classes and of many upper class and caste women, who shared the illusion of high position of women in India. To this date, the Report is considered to be a primary document on Indian women. The data regarding education, employment, political participation, sex ratio gave a very bleak picture of the real condition of women. Questions began to be raised as to whether this kind of situation was an indication of conditions for the last number of decades rather than a matter of immediate past. This resulted in doubts regarding impact of development policies. Thus when Prof. M.N. Srinivas wrote a booklet on the *'Changing Position of Indian Women'* in 1978, he did not write about women of India but pointed out that generalizations are impossible, because of considerable variations between rural and urban women, among classes and among different religious groups. The north of the Vindhyas and the south of the Vindhyas exhibit significant differences in culture and in production relations. Similarly Romila Thapar, the well known historian, remarks, "Within the Indian Sub-continent there have been infinite variations in the status of women, diverging according to cultural milieu, family structure, class, caste, property rights and morals." (quoted in *Women and Society*, p. 24) Likewise Sanskritist scholar Sukumari Bhattacharji points out the contradictory pictures emerging from the study of the Mahabharata. (Also refer to Prabhati Mukherjee).

As mentioned earlier *Towards Equality* led to questioning of the optimism about the status of women in society; the feminist movement particularly after the seventies reopened the women's question, however, with a different discourse. In order to understand the dichotomy in the status of women across class and caste axis and the challenges raised about the value structure which determined the status of women, the women's movements raised the issues such as control over sexuality, property, commodification of women, internalization of gender inequality and use of women by the Fundamentalist forces. It was realized that the increasing violence, both private and public, indicated significantly the reality of women's status.

The significance of this transformation in approach in the basic assessment of the status of women can be appreciated by looking at some empirical evidence. We will refer to three or four such cases which not merely raised fundamental questions about the real situation of women but also indicated the role of women's movement in questioning the academe: in the present situation, mainstream historians about their methodology, about the data sources and also about the interpretation of events.

III

One of the very crucial sources of information and insights into the status of women in contemporary society could be the various bench-mark events which have not only pointed out the dismal position of women but the role of women's action to raise the status of women. For the present purpose, I have selected four landmark events, they are Mathura Rape Case, Shah Bano Case, Sati incident and the issue of Reservation.

Mathura Rape Case

The Mathura Rape case has been considered as one of the main events that triggered off women's movement after the seventies. Rape is one of the most common and frequent of crimes against women, and rape in public places has begun to acquire attention. Mathura, a low-caste seventeen-year-old girl, was raped in the police station, while her brother and her boyfriend were waiting outside the chowki. Under pressure from the family and villagers, Mathura lodged a complaint against the policemen; they were acquitted by the Sessions Court, convicted at the High Court and later acquitted by the Supreme Court. The acquittal was based on flimsy grounds such as she had not protested, she was of questionable character, and so, was a loose woman. In 1980 the case was reopened through an open letter, written by four Professors of Law in Delhi, protesting against the Judgment of the Supreme Court. Though the judgment was not in favour of Mathura, it triggered off protest actions and raised some fundamental questions such as patriarchal-feudal attitude towards low caste women, the control over body, the mockery of need for evidence in such cases. Apart from these issues, the event led to the Women's Groups demanding action against the police and making the issue as main focus for the 8th March Women's Day. Later, cases of rape began to be on centre stage and rape as a punishment for challenging the authority of the family head or political power lord became visible as in case of Guntaben in Gujarat and Bhanwaribai in Rajasthan. (For details see Radhakumar). The events also led to the amendment in Rape Law. The agitation also led to questioning of control over sexuality, the poser that was never posed while evaluating the status of women.

Sati Case

Another significant event which was a tragic commentary on women's status in India, was the event of Roop Kanwar's self-immolation in 1987. Roop Kanwar had been married only a short while when her husband died. They had spent around six months together. When, after his death, it was announced that Roop would become sati, her own family members were not informed. Later evidence, which trickled down, indicated that it was murder rather than a voluntary act. She was dressed in her bridal finery, drugged and then put on the fire. The event shocked the country severely. Not that sati instances were not occurring in the country, but such blatant parading and forcing had not caught public attention. Finally, the *Chunari mahostsava* after ten days of the immolation was celebrated against protest from all the progressive sections of society. The incident was hailed as a great sacrifice, enshrining Roop to Satihood, thus glorifying human murder. The right wing tried to invoke the chivalric 'Rajput' tradition, the Sati temples and tried to encourage Hindu fundamentalism. Feminists protested against all these manifestations but the hidden agenda of majority-minority politics, caste and communal representation and the political footage which was provided, slowly came to light. The protestors were dubbed as modernists who were opposing the centuries' old tradition. When after a lot of pressure, the Government introduced a

Bill under which sati was defined as suicide, the first person to be punished was the woman herself, for attempting to committed suicide! Thus when a religious custom forces women to die on the funeral pyre of her husband and is glorified in the name of Hinduism, it simply indicates that the position of women in India needs to be studied more deeply. The valourisation of such women also brings to the forefront the inter-linkage between orthodoxy and gender subordination.

Shah Bano Case

Another crucial event that revealed the patriarchal overtones and the intertwining of the communal feelings in gender issues was the Shah Bano Case. On 23rd April 1985, the Supreme Court ruled that a 75-year-old woman Shah Bano was entitled to maintenance by her husband. Shah Bano was divorced by her husband after half a century of marriage. She filed a case of maintenance when her husband deserted her. The husband, who was an advocate, took shelter under the Muslim Personal Law and stated that the husband was not obliged to give maintenance. The judgment, on the one hand, upheld the women's right to get maintenance from her husband, and, on the other, tacitly suggested that the Muslim Personal Law was anti-woman and should be amended. It made a plea for Uniform Civil Code and suggested that Hindu Law was ideal! The controversies that followed and which are still alive led to divisions among the feminists as pro-Uniform Civil Code and pro-personal law groups. As far as the discussion on status of women is concerned, the issue pointed out the communalization of the problem, using gender as the main agent.

Reservation

The fourth significant event, which is dominating the political parties and the feminists, is the issue of Reservation in electoral seats. The issues of reservation and representation have been quite prominent in both the pre-and post-Independence periods. Since in the pre-Independence period women's movement was primarily motivated by principles of equal rights, they were against any scheme of reservation in election. After Independence, feminists were hopeful that equal opportunities would be created and they would not have to ask for reservation. Further, for a long time, feminists were more concerned with active politics rather than electoral politics, and so, the issue of representation was not so significant. However after nearly five decades the political participation of women is not only not substantial but, in fact, has been declining at times, which has led feminists to try to devise means of creating better opportunities for participation. As Radhakumar mentions in respect of reservation from *panchayat* upwards, "In the early days of the contemporary women's movement many of us used to scoff at the idea that women's representation in such bodies would actually further feminism; our view was that such representation automatically led to de-radicalization." Today many feminists are supporting the move and trying out ways to realize this representation. The change in approach has largely been due to the patriarchal attitude of the power-hungry parties, as they fear that with women's reservation their number and power will be drastically affected. In the majority rule political structures, number is very important and so all efforts are made to scuttle the bill for thirty-three percent reservation in the state assemblies as well as parliament. The severity of opposition has also been due to the success of women leadership in *Panchayat*, which is threatening the men. Recently it was debated that the political parties should themselves run women candidates proportionately as one method of enabling women to get representation. However, this move has also been ruled out, as this will affect the men candidates. Right now we are not at all optimistic about the introduction of the bill in Parliament.

Conclusion

The moot question is, what is the purpose of narrating these cases? As mentioned earlier, in order to understand the contemporary status of women, we have to go to traditional and non-traditional sources. The linear evolutionary model does not help in understanding the position of women. Firstly it conceives women as a homogeneous group, while in reality there are women who belong to different classes, castes, religions, regions and cultures. Many a time the mainstream refers to upper caste, middle and upper class women from majority groups. In order to get the real picture we have to look into the situation in poorer strata, women belonging to SCs and STs and women of the isolated regions. Secondly, the issues raised by the Feminist Movement point at not merely the oppression of women but also the underlying value system viz. patriarchal social structure governing the attitude. Thirdly, the feminist scholars have not only dealt with the oppression of women, but also with evidences of strengths and spaces carved out by women to assert their identity. Finally, the portrayal of contemporary women could be more clearly seen from overt evidences such as visibility through their participation in work, education, political power or their legal status and through media representation, as values suggested by the media are important sources. It is against this background that feminist historians talk about the role of social reformers or legislation or educational policy affecting women. Of course, much work is still to be done in this area. However, the beginnings have been made. Earlier it was thought that Indian women got equality very easily - on a platter. New evidence indicates that at times the veteran Congress leaders like Nehru, Rajendra Prasad or Vallabhbhai Patel were not considering gender question as a crucial one. Or nobody believed the left political parties were ignoring the gender issue. (Basu, Aparna *Laws*, 1997) Similarly there are a number of studies which try to reevaluate the role of political participation of women during the freedom struggle. Counteracting the earlier notion of invisibility of women or representing them merely in numbers, several attempts are made to assess women's participation in various mass movements, their predicaments, their own perceptions etc. (see Mehta, Sarkar, Forbes). Likewise the analysis of some of the issues taking a historical perspective and putting them in context has been one of the significant contributions of the social historians. Examination of some of the legal measures taken during colonial rule has been found to be serving the interests of the rulers or they have disregarded the cultural ethos of the Indian society. This is seen in the dealing with Rukmabai case or the analysis of runaway marriages reflecting the intertwining of caste, gender and class, the discussion of violence on abducted women manifested during the partition on the women of both the countries or the interrelationships between religious fundamentalism, gender and politics. (Sudhir Chandra, Jean D'cunha, Butalia, Sarkar).

In short, analysis of women in contemporary period is fundamentally different from the earlier approach in terms of methodology, data sources and theoretical perspective.

References

For details about the three cases viz. Mathura Rape case, Roop Kanwar's self immolation and Shah Bano Court case- the readers may refer to Radha Kumar, The History of Doing, Kali for women, New Delhi, 1993. As regards other points, a select bibliography in terms books and research-articles is given below. It may however be noted that some of the articles were merely presented at the seminars mentioned and are unpublished.

Books

1. Altekar, A.S. *The Position of Women in Hindu Civilization*, Motilal Banarsidas, Delhi, 1959.
2. Butalia Urvashi, *The Other side of Silence: Voices of the Partition*, Viking, London, 1998.
3. Desai, Neera, *Women in Modern India*, Vora and Co. Bombay, 1977.
4. Desai, Neera and Raj, Maithreyi Krishna, *Women and Society in India*, Ajantha Publication, 1987.
5. Dube, Leela, Leacock, Eleanor and Shirley Ardner (eds.) *Visibility and Power*, Oxford University Press, 1986.
6. Forbes, Geraldine *Women in Modern India*, Cambridge University Press, 1998.
7. Karlekar, Malvika, *Voices from Within*, Oxford University Press 1991.

8. Lerner, Gerda, *The Majority Finds its Past, Placing Women in History,* Oxford University Press 1979.
9. Mukherjee, Prabhati, *Hindu Women: Normative Models*, Orient Longman, 1978.
10. Thapan, Minakshi (ed.), *Embodiment: Essays on Gender and Identity*, Oxford University Press, 1997.
11. Sangari, Kumkum and Vaid, Sudesh (eds.), *Recasting Women: Essays in Colonial History*, Kali for Women, 1989.
12. Sarkar, Tanika, *Words to Win: The Making of Amar Jiban (A Modern Autobiography)*, Kali for Women, 1999.
13. The Government of India, *Towards Equality* (The Reports of Committee on the Status of Women in India) 1974.

2
Feminist Theology and Subordination of Women

Soonu J. Dhanjisha

The importance of religion can be seen in all the life experiences of people from different strata of society. Besides recommending values and attitudes it also governs the civil society. As all the religious texts are from the male perspective, they prevent men from seeing women's position as an alternative dimension. These texts are the product of rather totalitarian socio-economic and political systems. They reduced women's existence to one that was abstruse, cryptic and vague, which almost completely denied women from having any 'historical destiny'. Theology is the study of the existence of nature of God with regard to man's relationship to him. The word has come to denote a particular set of beliefs - Judaism, Islam, Christianity. Hinduism etc. Every theology has a context to the society, though it is hidden. Contextual theology is a conscious and deliberate attempt to practise theology from within the context of real life. Thus, all theology, even the most abstract, has been thought of in one sociological context or the other. Most of the theology has been contemplated in the isolated academia of only men. Women have hardly had (and even now hardly have) any say in them. Contextual theology is fully aware, right from the start that it is being conceived in and from a particular context or particular life-situation. Contextual theology is the discovery of the poor and the oppressed. Thus we have Liberation theology, Cultural theology, Black theology and Feminist theology, and in the Indian context, Dalit theology.

Feminist theology is theology that represents the experience of being a woman in 'a man's world', the experience of being deprived, marginalized and blamed as a woman. Other theology is for the most part masculine but that is never mentioned. The question of theology is a very powerful and pragmatic instrument for women's conception of God and herself, which was achieved by indoctrination – a deliberate attempt to suppress all possible criticism of the beliefs transmitted. According to Schofield, 'Indoctrination involves putting one line of argument so forcefully, so repeatedly, so uncompromisingly that one is unable even to consider any alternatives'. How otherwise can we explain the women of Rajasthan demanding *sati* as their right or those in Varanasi demonstrating against Deepa Mehta's "Water", which shows the plight of the Hindu widow? We also have Muslim women in favour of *burkha,* and Parsi women isolating themselves during their menses as it is considered impure.

Various theologies aspire to save women from being women, as if that in itself was the greatest sin. No distinction is made between sin and women. They had to be saved from such imagined evils as their dress, diet, habits and sexuality. In Christianity Eve is attributed with the original sin - regeneration and birth is considered as sinful. Hindus considered it a sin to kill, but godly to kill a widow as *sati*. Romila Thapar tracing the history of *sati* custom states that it was a symbol of aristocracy. Earlier a widow would lie on the funeral pyre of her husband and a male relative of her husband would raise her from it. It was in the later period that the burning of widows gained popularity. The Dharmasutras state that a woman's vision, her speech and her actions should be controlled by her husband. The *Arthashastra* is supposed to have shown leniency when husband's actions are controlled, for a wife must be beaten if she is impertinent and has a sharp tongue but only on her back and with a hand or a rope only.

Although women were allowed to become nuns and renounce earthly attachments in both Buddhism and Jainism, just as men were, they were regarded as inferior to the male monks. The *Dhammapada* directs that a Buddhist *bhikkuni* even of 100 years standing must bow low before a *bhikku* of 25 years, everyday. He also says that woman was devoid of spiritual knowledge and was a *kamini* (lust incarnate) who had to be rigidly controlled by the male. There are many denunciations of women and their evil desires to lure men away from the right path while there seems to be only one significant warning to women about the dangers of male sexuality. Goldman affirms that 'the texts and sermons of Buddhism and Jainism often stress so virulently negative a view of women as to make even the gynophobic elements in most Hindu texts seem rather mild'.

Though Islam gave a better status to women than what had existed earlier in Arabia, they were still bound and fettered. It was stated that a woman should not observe a fast (fast curbs sexuality) without the permission of her husband. A woman who evades the desire of her husband at night is cursed by the angels till she attends to him. Women, whose defiance was to be feared, were to be admonished and kept apart from the bed of a male. Women had to cover themselves in a *burkha*. This kind of seclusion of women left no field open to them. Unable even to have free social movement, they were kept at the mercy of their men for everything. One wonders whose interest and welfare were largely being served by these theologies. Theology was formulated against the background of all-pervasive superiority of men and of people in power. The oppression was and is so much a part of faith, both for men and women that it is only in the 19th century that they asked why? Why do these theologies state that:

Man dictates and woman agrees.

Man knows all and woman knows nothing.

Man disciplines and woman is disciplined.

Man imposes authority and woman loses her freedom.

Feminist theology therefore is called upon

(1) To answer the question for marginalizing women.

(2) To understand and interpret how women see a religion.

(3) To re-examine and re-state the nature of the faith.

My hypothesis shows that there is a definite link between theology and the role of women in that society and one can trace a parallel development through history. The excavations of Harappan civilization present evidence of mother goddess, the actual regeneration is shown through female figures. The function of mother goddess is completely independent of any male god. She was the wellspring of life. Though information about the society is scanty it has been pointed out that the quarters of Harappan workers show no evidence of status differentials among men and women. The skeletons and teeth show no difference in the diet of men and women. There was gender equality. During early Vedic period the two major goddesses were *Aditi* and *Prithvi*. They are described as 'holding the world in the womb' – *Visva garbha,* world bearer – *lokadharini*. They are not spouses of male gods and are not controlled by any. This attitude of gender equality can be seen in other contexts as well. Both girls and boys would undergo the initiation ceremony. Marriage was not obligatory to both sexes and widows remarried. Since women represented female energy, her presence at sacrificial rituals was essential. The wife was a partner (*ardhangini*) to her husband and his philosophical guide (*sahadharmini*).

There was a marked difference in the later Vedic period. A radically different one based on inequality and with a privileged position for men replaced the religious paradigm of the Great Goddess. With the philosophy that viewed worldly desires as evil, fertility and sexuality were considered evil and women were thought to be a distraction to men from the path of enlightenment. Goddesses had only secondary or marginal powers – mainly as wives, controlled by their spouses. In society, women's role in the spiritual domain was virtually wiped out. Girls were no longer educated and were married by the age of twelve to fourteen. They were stripped of their decision-making powers and were prevented from performing any religious rites. According to *Parasara Smrti,* "The sacrificer is learned, while his wife is ignorant". Women's body and specifically her menses and sexuality were defamed.

There was another interpretation of the feminine principle during 500 BCE. The universe was divided into two principles. Matter or *prakriti* was feminine and *Purush* was male. *Purush* came to be equated with *Atman* and *Prakiti* with *Maya*. The goal of *atman* was to be freed from the clutches of *maya*. Thus women came to be viewed as an impediment in the path of *moksha* and their position in society deteriorated still further. During the seventh century *Shakti* principle became prominent. Goddesses were personifications of the powers of male gods, like Brahma and Brahmani, Vishnu and Vaishnavi. Even Durga the most powerful goddess was the *Shakti* of all gods put together. They no longer had any independent entity. Women during this period were deprived of any independent role in the society. They were completely under the domination of men. Thus the inbred assurance of male superiority - physical, emotional and intellectual - was promulgated.

A definite parallel can be seen between feminist theology and women's role in society. Whenever there is a positive theology with an independent existence, there is a larger role for women in that society as a mother, educator and worker. When goddesses have less independent function and control, there is subordination of women by men. While women appear to have been active early in the first millennium BCE, their participation was eclipsed in the later periods. Eventually the religious traditions of all the religions imposed constraints on women. It is difficult to say whether theology influenced the social structure more or vice versa. However it is certain that no social structure is independent of its theology. Feminist view of theology thus becomes an important source for the study of women's history. An important contribution of women's self-study is to show that these theologies are men's view only. It is only a partial view, and although it is presented as the whole, it is false.

References

1 Altekar A. S., *The Position of Women in Hindu Civilization: From Prehistoric Time to the Present Day,* Motilal Banarsidas, Delhi, (1938) 1962.

2. Ananda Sri, "Religio-cultural Approach to the Gender problems in India", *Dharma Vol. XII, no. 4.* Dharma Research Association, Bangalore, 1988.

3. Brown, C. M., *God as Mother: A Feminine Theology in India.* Claude Stark and Company, Hardford, 1974.

4. Kosambi D. D. *Ancient India: A History of its Culture and Civilization,* Random House, New York, 1974.

5. Pandharipande, R., "Spiritual Dimensions of Fertility Cult and Power Woman", *Dharma. Vol. XII, no. 3,* Dharma Research Association, Bangalore, 1988.

6. Syed Maududi, *Purdah and the Status of Women in Islam,* Tr. Al-Ash Ari, Markagi Maktaba Islamic, Delhi, 1976.

7. Thottakara, Augustine, (ed.) *Women and Worship: Perspective from World Religions,* Dharmaram Publication, Bangalore, 2000.

3

The Problems in Laws Faced by the Muslim Women of India

Dr. Ramala N. Baxamusa

Introduction

The economic liberalization in Indian has resulted in almost all the lower and the lower middle class women having to bear the brunt of socio-economic oppression. All women have to face the problems caused by severe inflation. Changes in production lines and wide scale privatization have rendered many men and women jobless. This has created tension in the house as women are pushed into the labour market to make ends meet. The change of roles results many times in breaking of marriages. The existing discrepancies of the personal laws of most of the religious groups do most injustice to women. One finds that as Islamic law in India has faced historic changes the Muslim women have to suffer the most.

The statistical profile shows that in India Muslims form nearly 12.14 percent of the population, of which 35 per cent is in urban areas and 4.24 per cent rural (Census 1992). The Muslims are the largest minority in India. The sex ratio is 925 female to 1000 males. Out of the 21 states of India, Kerala, West Bengal, U.P., Lakshawdeep, Assam, and Bihar have a higher Muslim population. In West Bengal 95 per cent and in Kerala 85 per cent of Muslim women live in rural areas while in Maharashtra 66 per cent of the Muslim women population is urban. (Census 1981 (1985).

The aim of this paper is to trace how the present personal laws have evolved. Are all the Muslim women living in India governed by the same law? Why is there no move to help women with their problems? To try and understand some of the problems, a brief survey is made of the way in which law evolved, and the changes that such laws underwent over time.

Pre-Islamic laws denied women most rights, for women were regarded as a commodity. Before Prophet Mohammad, Arabia was occupied largely by pastoral Bedouin tribes, and by some merchants, living in towns. In both, women were not given importance.

A woman had no right to inheritance from her parents or husbands. After the death of the husband the wives became the property of the stepsons. He either married her or gave her in marriage to others. It was not essential to be married before having children. Female infanticide was apparently common, for Arabs generally did not welcome daughters – a fairly common custom was burial of daughters alive in sand. In the pre-Islamic days there was no restriction on number of wives. On an average a Qurayshi man had ten wives. When marriage took place the father / brother / cousin got bride price from the husband. During *jahiliyah* right to divorce remained only with men. Incest marriage was not permitted, but cousins' marriages were allowed.

When Prophet Mohammed destroyed the tribal Gods and spread Islam in the 7th century, there was a revolutionary change regarding the position of women. For the first time she was treated on par with the men as a human being. Her rights were not equal to the menfolk but she received half of what the men received. A woman was permitted rights over her property (earned / inherited); if she wanted she could use her wealth for herself and her husband but the husband had no right to demand, use or interfere with her property. The Quran insisted that it was the duty of her husband to look after her and thus he had some rights over her. Thus he could divorce her without her permission but she was allowed *khul'a* only with her permission; this was due to the condition during that period.

The Prophet disapproved of female infanticide, and issued moral restrictions on the killing of female children. Restrictions were put on the right to marry. A man was permitted to marry only four wives but only when there was war and widow / orphans needed to be protected. Secondly they were supposed to have the capacity to treat all wives uniformly. The Quran opposed marriage with the stepmother, calling it incest and stopped it. Marriage to any blood relatives was not permitted but marriage to adopted son's wife or daughter was allowed.

The Quran insisted that no bride price was to be paid to the parents. But to solemnize the marriage the husband would have to pay the wife *Mahr* which was to be an amount that the wife could ask for, or that which was equivalent to the economic status of the woman. Islam permitted the tribal custom of approval of the parents but also insisted on that of the girl. Quran put restrictions on men divorcing women and insisted that at least a three-month waiting period was necessary before a divorce was finalized. It also insisted that there was necessity for arbitration from both sides. The Quran gave women right to divorce i.e., *Khul'a*. The Quran said that divorce was bad but it was permitted, as it did not want society to break. To give paternal right to children Islam insisted on marriage. During this period purdah did not exist.

After the death of Prophet Mohammed, and the splitting up of his followers into the two major groups of Shia and Sunni, schools of jurisprudence began to emerge. The Sunnis emphasised *Qiyas* (consensus) and *ijma* (analogy) as the basis of law. However, the source of law was understood by both to be the Quran and the Hadis, the sayings of the Prophet. When the Muslim empire expanded different geographical, racial, and cultural traditions embraced Islam; thus their way of looking at the problems differed.

All this resulted in the birth of various schools of Islamic Sunni and Shiite Jurisprudence. These finally coalesced broadly into four Sunni Schools - Hanifi, Maliki, Hanbali and Shafi. The three Shiite schools are Ithna Ashari, Ismaili and Fatimi. As the founders lived in various places such as Medina, Mecca, Kufa, (Iraq) and Misar (Egypt) and Persia, the laws tended to incorporate the local customs as well. This resulted in different interpretations of the laws, resulting in position of women to vary. It is a well-known fact that Imam Abu Hanifi and Imam Shafi were more liberal in their approach as they lived in Iraq and Egypt respectively, which makes their laws progressive. According to Abu Zayd, Imam Hanifi was a liberal, Imam Shafi a moderate, Imam Maliki a conservative, and Imam Hambal rigid and orthodox (Engineer 1992, p8).

The Shiite jurisprudence were the Ithna Ashari from Persia and the Ismaili from Yemen. There was no unity between different schools. Shiites were influenced by Sunni thought, but the Sunnis never united on issues. However, the amalgam of cultures and traditions expressed in such schools of jurisprudence often accepted the earlier traditions of, in particular, Arabia and Persia, especially with regard to women, thus affecting the real position of women in Islam. The Persian culture brought the concept of purdah and this has today resulted in putting women behind the veil and in harems.

It is to be remembered that the Sharia and the Hadis are not the words of Quran or what the Prophet himself spoke but the words of his companions - how they understood these words. There are possibilities that human factors are involved and human beings can err. Until the seventh and the eighth Islamic centuries there were a few changes, but in the later period the law has become very rigid.

The triple *talaq,* which is affecting women most, is the product of this period. The Shafi Sunni school and all the Shiite schools do not approve of this method of talaq. The followers of the Hanifi School, which is 80 per cent in India, believe that though the Quran is not supporting it, they still will use it. According to them Hazrat Umar had introduced the pre Islamic Triple talaq in one sitting as punishment to men who unwisely divorced their wives. Today this practice is going against a woman, leaving her at the mercy of a man without any security. In recent times, one does come across some important changes in Muslim Laws in a few Islamic and non-Islamic countries supporting the Islamic Laws for Muslim women. This is primarily due to the changes that have taken place in Turkey, for, until 1924, due to the rule in Turkey of the Khalifa, Islamic laws had become static.

When the Muslim Empire was lost in Turkey to the French they used the Swiss Code to solve the problems of the women. New laws were made in favour of women. To save the Islamic Laws the Ulema then agreed to make changes within the Islamic framework. They used the liberal Islamic laws and thus change in the Islamic laws within Islamic framework began. One finds that today in Islamic and the non-Islamic countries to serve the women population many changes have been introduced but one still finds that changes are comparatively very slow. The Muslim women had fought battles in the beginning of the century but today their movement is very slow and thus still their problems are not solved. Now in many countries a beginning has been made and there are hopes that women's voices shall be heard. (Engineer 1992, p.8)

While Islamic jurisprudence was on the whole codified outside India, they were brought into India as well. However though Muslims of the world may follow a similar religion they are very much different culturally. One finds that Indian Muslims are, in custom and behaviour, much closer to the Hindus of India than the Muslims of other countries. In India too one finds that in each region the Muslim population is not homogeneous. The Muslim population is divided into various sects depending on the history of their origin. They are affiliated to various religions missionaries, having different occupation resulting in division into various socio-economic positions, resulting in numerous sects. Thus all Muslim women are not alike, though all are governed by their Islamic school of law i.e. their jurisprudence.

Some 80 per cent of the Indian Muslims are Sunni, while the rest are Shia, a majority of whom believe in the Ithna Ashari School while the rest are the Ismailis. The study of the judicial schools is important; this has been dealt with earlier. In India till 1920s the Catchy Memon and the Ismaili Khoja in relation with women's inheritance used the Hindu laws. Although Islam talks of brotherhood and social and religious equality, in reality here too, like in all other religions of India, there was stratification into various heterogeneous sects. Each group has its traditional occupation, which is now undergoing change as a result of industrialization and education. These sects generally maintain endogamous marriage rules and try and observe their separate sect identity.

A brief legal history of the Muslim period would help us to assess the changes that were brought about by the British. There is no documentary history about Muslim period. The Sultanate as well as the Mughal used the Hanifi laws for all Muslims but the Hindus were governed by their own laws. The Shites in private used their own Shiite laws but if caught had to suffer. (Fyzee 1972).

In 1772, during the Governor-Generalship of Warren Hastings, changes were made in the legal structure then prevalent in Bengal, as a result of which the Hazrat Adalat and the Nizamat Adalats were introduced. Warren Hastings said that in the three presidencies, in question of succession, special property or females divorce, dowers, adoption dower, etc, the personal law of both Hindus and Muslims was to be used. However it was stated in 1887 that local customs shall be applicable to the party even if it goes against the personal laws. (Mohammed 1965).

In 1847 a Shiite Khoja daughter asked for her inheritance right, and a childless widow from the Memon community asked for her inheritance right according to Islamic personal law. As the British were not affected by the judgment, they took the male side and said that Hindu law governed these sects, and thus no inheritance would be given to the women. In contrast to this, in Kerala where matriarchal system existed, in the name of Islamic Law women were deprived of their right and patriarchal system was established. Law, especially personal law, thus became a weapon which could be used to keep women at the mercy of their men. So, for example, though women enjoyed inheritance right, land was never given to them in Northern India and this is done even today.

Many such irresponsible judgments all over India divided the Muslim Jamats of many sects. Muslim women began to rise in anger, perhaps in reaction to the fact that, by the 1930's, in the Western world women's movement was expanding. In the Islamic countries, there was demand for change to use only the Quranic Islamic laws. All this boosted Muslim women's movement in India. The Ulema fearing that movement may go out of control asked the British to pass the Sharia Act 1937. This Act tried to codify the Islamic laws and replace the use of customary laws. This well-codified Act of the Ulema was at the last moment changed due to interference of Mr. Jinnah. He succeeded in interfering and he wiped out the codification of the law. All the different Muslim Jamats were permitted to use their specific school. Thus the real purpose of Uniform Sharia act was defeated and all later efforts were in vain, and even today the Muslim law remains not codified.

Though women had the right to divorce, in practice the British courts did not permit many women to take divorce. Therefore Muslim women converted to Hindus. As Islam believes that marriage of non-Muslim to a Muslim is null and void many women got divorce. To avoid further conversion the Muslim Ulema with the British Government drafted the Dissolution of Marriage Bill, which was uniform for all Muslims. It was codified and the different Jamats were not permitted to use their own schools of law. This was real progress, but unfortunately these laws give protection to men and deprive women of what is theirs. Women who approach court lose their right to residence and Mahr. Thus the British (Anglo) personal Law is today's Muslim Personal Law where some wrong anti-Islamic practices are also accepted. (Baxamusa 1983).

Since 1947 there is not much change. Even though the Ulema were aware that in many cases the existing Islamic laws were going against the true Islamic practices they did not bringing about change. In Northern India even today the daughters are not given land as a right in their father's property. When partition brought lots of enmity between the two communities the political leaders did not insist on updating the Muslim Law. The leaders asked for protection to Islamic law calling it secret and demanded a promise that no change would be introduced by the Constitution and there would be no Uniform Civil code. Therefore in 1950 a promise was given by the Congress that no change would be brought in without the sanction of the Muslims. But the Constitution also adopted at the same time Article 35 (now Article 44) directing the State to endeavor to secure a Uniform Civil Code later when time was right (Baxamusa 1977).

In the 1950-60's in India there was hardly any demand for change in Islamic laws. Though the same period saw the passing of the Special Marriage and Succession Act (1952) and the Hindu Code Bill (1955), no attempt was made to update Muslim laws. Progressive Muslims demanded stoppage of polygamy when in 1961 in Pakistan, (where the similar Anglo Mohammedan Personal law had existed) the Family Code Bill was introduced which put restriction on polygamy and gave right to orphans. This demand was interpreted as interference with Islam. Seminars were organized where a number of views were expressed. A few Muslim lawyers and social workers spoke in favour of change in the personal laws. They were supported by the Ulema of Deoband, Rajkotla, Patna, and Hyderabad, who agreed to reforms in the Muslim law within Islamic framework. During this time the atmosphere was pro-change but there was insistence that it should be within the Islamic framework.

In this period A. B. Shah and Hamid Dalvi criticized the Islamic law that it did not give equal rights to women. Therefore through the platform of the Indian Secular Society and the Satyashodak Mandal, they asked for a Uniform Civil Code Bill. The Congress government in 1968 organized a seminar in Delhi to discuss Uniform Civil Code. In 1967 the Jan Sangh passed a resolution for Indianization. They demanded that different religions in India should merge with ancient Indian culture and they should all support the uniform civil code bill. Muslims arranged a seminar in Aligarh. The press covered the debate extensively. During this period many secularists, communists and liberals supported social reforms but the Ulema refused to accept the Uniform Civil Code and all the jurists from various schools who had never united, joined hands. (Engineer 1987) The Ulema of different Jamats organized conventions and seminars to appose UCL. They joined hands with the RSS and also the Christian Clergy to oppose the Uniform Civil Code.

In 1971 the Bharatiya Jan Sangh Party election manifesto talked of 10 points to unify India. They also talked of the Uniform Civil Code based on Hindu dharma. In 1972 the Law Institute organized a seminar in Delhi. Here for the first time problems of women like triple divorce was discussed. (Mohammed1986) However thereafter the only discussions were on what should be done to save Islam. This brought a rift between the Hindus and Muslims. In 1972 the Ulema organized a convention in Bombay and asked the Government not to interfere directly or indirectly. With the help of Indira Gandhi in 1972 All India Muslim Personal Law Board (MPLB) was constituted. Their work was to protect Sharia. (Baxamusa 1997).

A Uniform Civil Code Bill–discussion became so important the problems of women were put aside. A demand was put to delete Article 44 so that the Uniform bill was never introduced. A Muslim women's seminar was organized to oppose change; they said all was fine. Faced with opposition from various groups, the progressives also became silent, and began to agree that they too wanted change within the Islamic system. It was declared that the Government should wait until the Muslims themselves demanded change. The issues concerning women were left unanswered and Muslim women's condition deteriorated. In 1983, Shanaz Sheikh was given oral talaq. A case was filed in the Supreme Court. There was opposition from the MPLB but nothing happened, as the case did not come for hearing.

This has remained a constant problem, for while suits are filed, the cases are often settled out of court, and so do not come up for hearing. In Kerala maintenance cases were filed and many Muslim women were given maintenance after divorce. The Shah Bano case became famous for she demanded maintenance from her husband in 1981. The judgment that was finally given went against Shah Bano.

The M. P. L. B. which intervened in the case objected to the Supreme Court judgment and described it as gross interference of the Supreme Court in the Muslims' affairs. Insecurity among the Muslims moved them to support M.P.L.B. to recover its lost prestige. Many women in seminars made speeches that they were not interested in taking maintenance from their divorced husbands.

Zoya Hasan in April 1986 of CPI was the first Muslim woman to organize a conference of progressive Muslim Women in Delhi. Many like-minded Muslims from all over India attended.

The M. P.L.B. lobby was strong, and the Congress was not interested in losing votes. Rajiv Gandhi gave in to the demands of the Muslims in 1986 and exempted all Muslim Women from the purview of section 125 of the CrPc. The ironically named Muslim Women's Bill to protect the Rights of Women from Divorce, in reality took away even what the Quran gave her. As M.P.L.B. was the only body representing the major Jamats in India, eyes were turned to them to wake up and do something to save their women.

In 1990's a group of social workers and lawyers formulated a reformed Nikha-Nama. This was discussed with ulema and corrected to make the reformed Nikha-nama more Islamic, but at the same time give solution to existing problems faced by women. This was presented to The Personal Law Board, but no action has been taken.

In the Tilhari case government did not accept triple talaq and questioned the validity of triple talaq. This resulted in lots of discussion among Muslims and others, something that has surfaced again in recent days.

In the 90's after a period of silence, movement for change started springing up among the Indian, Muslims and there were seminars organized all over India in North and South, to discuss the Muslim Women's problems; triple talaq, Polygamy, mahr, divorce etc.

In 1999 a women's group Awaza Nisva organized two all India level seminars to discuss how to use the Islamic laws and bring change which could be beneficial to women and children. They invited the MPLB to consider and think about change.

In 1999 a women's group Awaza Nisva had organized seminars so that there is today growth of discussion in Urdu press on reforms and Nikha-Nama. After a good discussion among the Muslim Social workers from all over India a committee was set up to pressurize the State and Centre to ask the M.P. L.B. to draft social change to help the suffering Muslim women.

The above sequence of events has played an important part in making the issues of change a very sensitive one. To day this has become an identity issue. Ulema instead of correcting the wrong practices is leading them away form the correct path.

One has seen that a beginning has been made and this will continue. One hopes that new people will join the movement and surely taking notice of the plight of poor women the Muslim Personal Law Board will make changes within the Islamic framework and save the women.

References

1. Baxamusa R. M. "Muslim Women's of Bombay", R.C.W.S.S.N.D.T. University Mimeograph, Bombay, 1982.
2. Baxamusa R. M. "The Legal Status of Muslim Women.", R.C.W.S. S.N.D.T. University, Bombay, 1983.
3. Baxamusa R. M."The Shah Bano Controversy." Orient Longman, Hyderabad, 1998.
4. Engineer A.A. "The Shah Bano Controversy." Orient Longman, Hyderabad, 1987.
5. Baxamusa R. M. "The Rights of Women in Islam". Sterling Publishers Pvt. Ltd, Delhi, 1954.
6. Fyzee A.A.A. "Outline of Muhammadan Law." Oxford University Press, Delhi 1954.
7. Mahmood T. "The Muslim Personal Law. Role of the State." Vikas, Delhi, 1977

4

A Gender Approach to the Smrti of Manu

Ms. Archana Mishra

Of utmost antiquity and authority, the *Manusmrti* has come in for severe criticism from the subaltern section of Hindu society, so much so that in 1927 a copy of the text was ceremoniously cremated at Mahad by Dr. B.R. Ambedkar as a symbolic act of rejecting its sanctity as a source of law, being based on inequality between man and man and allowing exploitation of man by man in the name of 'sacred law'. Interestingly, though the text contains numerous verses now regarded as patently anti-women, the feminist critique goes back to little beyond the 80s of the last century, while historiography on women of early India was undertaken as early as the middle of the 19th century. This decisively demonstrates the fact that the content of a source of history is as important as the context in which it is viewed, and with every change in the latter, a new meaning and interpretation will emerge, enriching our understanding of the past and exemplifying the well-known dictum of Carr about history as the 'dialogue between the past and the present'.

Whether revered or reviled, the *Smrti* of Manu remains one of the finest embodiments of classical Hindu law and of fundamental importance in any study of ancient Indian law. Irrespective of the acrimonious debates its contents have evoked, its overbearing importance as a sociological and religious text exercising widespread influence can hardly be denied. Perhaps, our problem is rooted in equating the English term 'law' with the Sanskrit term '*dharma*', which is much wider in scope and application. Equality as a concept governing human relationships can hardly be expected from a text compiled about 2000 years ago. In the face of sharp social stratification, the concept of '*dharma*' in its day-to-day application was concerned with the individual in accordance with his station in life, which would hardly ever be identical for all members of the society. Notwithstanding this assumed basis for application of the principle of inequality between man and man, it remained restricted only to men because women of all classes and castes have everywhere been bracketed and viewed as a single social category. This quintessential distinction between man and woman in prescription of their respective rights and disabilities brings us to the need to re-examine the text with a gender approach.

Gender as a category of historical analysis entails the construction of the masculine and the feminine in a given society at a given time and helps in comprehending the set of relationships between the two in terms of rights and restrictions involved for each. Gender identity is a social construction imposed upon a sexed body and is so constituted as to privilege those that lay down the definitions and explanations of categories and injunctions involved. The entire exercise is geared to the fulfilment of goals and ideals visualized at moral, philosophical and even metaphysical levels so as to give a cohesive and comprehensive appearance to the culture that is created in the process. The *Smrti* of Manu that represents a distinctive stage in the development of Indian culture should be viewed not only in terms of verses praising and abusing women, but also in terms of the goals and ideals it sets out for the social order, and its attempt to accommodate a variety of social formations that contributed to its content, a process that naturally contributed elements of contradiction.

Falling in the category of metrical *Smrtis*, Buhler designates the *Manusmrti* as "Bhrgu's version of the Institutes of Sacred law proclaimed by Manu".[1] He presumed the *Manava Dharmasastra* to be the origin of the available text.[2] An aura of divinity has usually surrounded such metrical *Smrtis*. "These peculiarities are particularly marked in the *Manava Dharmasastra* where the whole first chapter is devoted to the purpose of showing the mighty scope of the book and of setting forth its divine origin as well as the manner in which it is revealed to mankind."[3] Most authorities place the compilation of this text in the bracket BC 200 – AD 200, and in this context Kane was guided by the fact that most authors of *Dharmasastra* works from the second century AD give credence to Manu's views.[4] Thus the available *Smrti* is not a homogeneous text but a mass of floating customs and traditions put together in the course of several centuries. What has been handed down is the edited and re-edited version of metrical verses compiled by the Brahmanas of the Bhrgu school who were hardly concerned, as we now are, with critically editing the material by way of separating earlier and later date layers and various opinions attributed to Manu, even if contradictory. Evoking a deep sense of awe and veneration as it did, the name of Manu imparted authority and sanctity to practices and beliefs of diverse origins, but attributed to him. Far from being an individual in flesh and blood, Manu had already acquired mythical dimensions, as reflected in the belief of multiple Manus recorded not only in the text itself, but in the *Gita* as well.[5] Kurundkar has rightly explained "the name of Manu tends to place a protective cover even around the basest of verses in the book".[6] This is what one would call the process of legitimizing and sanctifying a wide variety of social attitudes, customs and beliefs, the emerging picture being that of a social order naturally characterized by conflicting doctrines. A particular set of verses could be collected to condemn Manu as anti-*Sudra* or anti-woman or to prove him as pro-*Sudra* or pro-woman. Altekar illustrated this dichotomy by pointing out Manu's prescriptions to the effect that a husband should wait for a long time in order to be sure that his wife is barren and also permitting her supersession on the flimsy ground of being disagreeable.[7] As it is nearly impossible to identify and separate the various layers that went into the making of the *Manusmrti*, obtaining a cohesive and convincing picture of contemporary social reality is bound to fail, more so when we realise that the traditions finding place in the final compilation were separated from each other not only in terms of time, but distance as well.

Given this situation, even a statistical approach in terms of locating and counting the number of verses on a point and attempting to arrive at some generalization may hardly be possible.[8] All that one can attempt is to classify available verses in terms of some broad general categories to highlight the understanding that there is always a middle ground in between the extremes for which Manu has been condemned or praised. This precisely is the modest purpose of the present paper.

The patriarchal nature of the text can be seen reflected in a series of verses in Chapters III and IV, where women have been viewed most favourably, but only within the familial context.

> "Women must be honoured and adorned by their fathers, brothers, husbands and brothers-in law, who desire [their own] welfare." (III, 55)
>
> "Where women are honoured there the gods are pleased; but where they are not honoured, no sacred rite yields rewards." (III, 56)
>
> "Where the female relations live in grief, the family soon wholly perishes; but that family where they are not unhappy, ever prospers." (III, 57)
>
> "The houses on which female relations, not being duly honoured, pronounce a curse, perish completely, as if destroyed by magic." (III, 48)
>
> "Infants, aged, poor, sick men must be considered as men of the middle sphere; the eldest brother as equal to one's father, one's wife and one's son as one's own body." (IV, 184)

> "One's daughter as the highest object of tenderness; hence if one is offended by [any one of] these, one must bear it without resentment."

A few more such verses could be cited, but these perhaps suffice to bring home the nature and content of the prescriptions projecting women in a favourable light. In the first verse, all male relatives are enjoined to honour and adorn women related to them in various capacities, so as to earn their own welfare, while in the second the pleasure and displeasure of the gods is believed to depend on the way a family treats its women. The third verse also echoes this view indirectly, while the fourth brings home the power of a curse by grief-stricken women. In the last two verses the wife has been proclaimed part of the husband's body, and he is ordained to treat the daughter with the highest tenderness. Together, the verses do indicate that a section of society, even if patriarchal in nature and functioning, offered a distinct place of dignity and worth to its women in their familial roles. The verses reflect the ideals envisaged by the society or a section thereof, as consequences for disregarding them have been conceived at the divine level.

Now we may switch over to the duties of women with the family. In tune with the patriarchal trend of the text, women of all ages and communities are enjoined to remain subjected to the authority of males in the family.

> "By a girl, by a young woman and even by an aged one, nothing must be done independently even in her own house." (V, 147)

> "In childhood, a female must be subject to her father, in youth to her husband, when her lord is dead to her sons, a woman must never be independent." (V, 148)

This idea of absolute subjection is reaffirmed in the individual role of woman as wife and widow:

> "Though destitute of virtue, or seeking pleasure [elsewhere] or devoid of good qualities, [yet] a husband must be constantly worshipped as a god by a faithful wife." (V, 154)

> "Him to whom her father may give her, or her brother with the father's permission, she shall obey as long as he lives, and when he is dead, she must not insult [his memory]." (V, 151)

However the father has been entrusted with the duty of marrying the maiden only to a man of good qualities and the husband is taught to treat his wife as a divine gift:

> "But the maiden, though marriageable, should rather stop in [the father's] house until death, than he should ever give her to a man destitute of good qualities." (IX, 89)

> "The husband received his wife from the gods [he does not wed her] according to his own will; doing what is agreeable to the gods he must always support her [while she is] faithful." (IX, 101)

Along with the emphasis on wifely fidelity as seen in the verses above, that of the husband towards the wife has been proclaimed in equally emphatic terms:

> " 'Let mutual fidelity continue until death' this may be considered as the summary of the highest law for husband and wife." (IX, 101)

For violating wifely duty or treating the parental family as much superior to that of the husband's, the injunction prescribed is inhuman and has rightly been condemned by feminists. However, equally terrible, if not identical punishment has been prescribed for the male offender, as can be seen in the verses below:

> "If a wife, proud of the greatness of her relatives or [her own] excellence, violates the duty which she owes to her lord, the King shall cause her to be devoured by dogs in a place frequented by many." (VIII, 371)

> "Let him cause the male offender to be burnt on a red-hot iron bed; they shall put logs under it until the sinner is burnt to death." (VIII, 372)

The fact that the verses appear sequentially together makes it clear that their author compiler viewed infidelity in conjugal relations on either part as the most reprehensible among crimes, meriting prohibitive punishment. Elsewhere also we find that guarding of women and punishing male offenders in an exemplary manner is repeated:

> "Men who commit adultery with the wives of others, the King shall cause to be marked by punishments which cause terror and afterwards banish." (VIII, 352)
>
> "A man who is not a Brahman ought to suffer death for adultery: for the wives of all the four castes must always be carefully guarded." (VIII, 359)

Subjection of women to their male relatives or authorities in any patriarchal society is understandable, but their treatment in terms of a commodity bracketed with other such items, or their condemnation in explicit terms as evil by nature clearly reflects the hand of a misogynist in the composition of the text. Let us first take verses defining the evil nature of women.

> "It is in the nature of women to seduce men in this [world] for that reason the wise are never unguarded in [the company of] females." (II, 213)
>
> "For women are able to lead astray in this world not only a fool, but even a learned man, and [to make] him a slave of desire and anger." (II, 214)

However, the next verse is significant and though it could be interpreted as anti-woman, yet it does not seem so explicitly.

"One should not sit in a lonely place with one's mother, sister or daughter: for the senses are powerful and master even a learned man." (II, 215)

It is needless to explain that this factor of 'senses are power' could be applicable to both the sexes, but the mention to 'learned man' indicates the emphasis. This ambivalence of attitude or even cases of clear contradiction could be located in the commodity concept as well.

> "Chariots and horses, elephants, parasols, money, grain, cattle, women, all sorts of [marketable] goods and

> valueless metals belong to him who takes them [singly] conquering [the possessor]." (VII, 96)

> "A wife, a son, and a slave, these three are declared to have no property: the wealth which they earn is [acquired] for him to whom they belong." (VIII, 416)

No doubt, here the wife has been bracketed with son and slave, showing that she has mot been singled out for subjection to the patriarch, and the commodity concept is clear. Yet, in another context, it is specifically laid down that no gratuity could be accepted by a father for his daughter,

> "for a man who through avarice takes a gratuity is a seller of his offspring." (III, 51)

Again, related to this, but contrary to the verse cited above, in the injunction

> "But those male relations who, in their folly, live on the separate property of women [i.e. 'appropriate], the beasts of burden, carriages and clothes of women, commit sin and will sink into hell." (III, 52)

Finally, we may take up verses in which women figure and have been bracketed with men of certain categories, but the rational basis thereof is not easy to establish.

> "Way must be made for a man in a carriage, for one who is above ninety years old, for one diseased, for the carrier of a burden, for a woman, for a *snataka*, for the king and for a bridegroom." (II, 138)

> "Let him not eat in the company of his wife, nor look at her, while she eats, sneezes, yawns or sits at her ease." (IV, 43)

> "A Brahman must never eat a dinner given at a sacrifice that is offered by one who is not a *srotriya*, by one who sacrifices for a multitude of men, by a woman or by a eunuch." (IV, 205)

> "Nor [food] given without due respect; nor [that which contains] meat eaten for no sacred purpose, nor [that given] by a female who has no male [relatives], nor the food of an enemy, nor that [given] by the lord of a town,

nor that [given] by outcastes, nor that on which anybody has sneezed." (IV, 213)

"Nor [the food given] by those who knowingly bear with paramours [of their wives] and by those who in all matters are ruled by women, nor food [given by men] whose ten days of impurity on account of death have not passed, nor that which is unpalatable." (IV, 217)

One thing very clearly emerging from the above provisions is that they relate to women as a single category, irrespective of the class or station in life, whereas men figure as multiple categories. Though this is true of any text composed to enshrine patriarchal values, hierarchy in terms of caste / kinship has been maintained among otherwise single category women elsewhere in the text (II, 132; II, 210; VIII, 385). These internal variations forming the basis of injunctions reflect the attempt of the Brahmanical elite male to assert his supreme position in society vis-à-vis other males and all the females. But again, a closer look at the above verses will show that, in place of building a rational basis for asserting primacy of the elite male, the composers of these verses merely indulged in equating categories of people that had nothing even remotely in common, or prescribed conditions which would defy all attempts at applications. One fails to comprehend, for example, the bracketing of a female devoid of male relatives, the lord of a town, and an outcaste. Again, how the Brahman guest was to verify the credentials of a host bearing with paramours of his wife or being ruled by women in the family is difficult to understand. Also, the right to passage on priority basis has been given to all women along with *snatakas* and kings, which reflects an attempt to codify different traditions without attempting to evolve any cohesion among the categories involved. Finally, one also fails to understand the prohibition to eat in the company of one's wife or to look at her while she eats, sneezes, yawns or sits at ease. Such provisions have to be seen juxtaposed with far more clear and quite general provisions, such as

"In that family where the husband is pleased with his wife and wife her husband, happiness will assuredly be lasting." (III, 60)

This is not to say that, the clearer the provision, the greater its validity, and the closer to reality its contents. This is only to point out that verses composed with a view to incorporating traditions of diverse origins tend to be illogical and incomprehensible at the hands of a compiler / editor wanting to evolve an artificial order out of them, so as to be in tune with the prevailing ideology in the society and time from which he happened to come.

Thus in the final analysis one could say that any approach to studying the text has to take into account the multiple layers, representing diverse traditions that originated in societies separated from each other in terms of time as well as space, lying embedded in the body of the text in such a manner that any generalization has to be based on some selected set of verses. These would then have to exclude or downplay other verses that either modify or contradict these selected verses. The *Smrti* of Manu must be seen in the totality of the situations of its origin and evolution and in association with other contemporary sources.

References

1. *The Sacred Books of the East,* vol. XXV, Clarendon Press, Oxford, 1886, Introduction, p. xi.
2. *Ibid.*, p. xiii.
3. *Ibid.*, pp. xi-xii.
4. P.V. Kane, *History of the Dharmasastra*, Vol. I, p. 148.
5. *Manu*, I.36; *The Gita*, X.6
6. Narhar Kurundkar, *Manusmrti: Contemporary Thoughts*, translated from Marathi by Madhukar Deshpande, Popular Prakashan, Bombay, 1993,p. viii.
7. A.S. Altekar, *The Position of Women in the Hindu Civilization*, p. 107, footnote.
8. There are any number of studies done on the *Manusmrti* which could be cited, quoted from and discussed, but none has viewed the text in terms of its true nature, evolution and plurality of authorship, with the result that they fail to offer satisfactory explanations and interpretations of the data derived. Hence taking them up would only add to the length of the paper.

5

Avantisundari—A Learned Woman of Early India

Kamal Abhyankar

This short paper aims at introducing *Avantisundari*, a little known but brilliant and learned woman of the 10th century AD. Further, this essay seeks to highlight the socio-cultural milieu of that time.

Avanti was the wife of Rajasekhar, the poet, dramatist, poetician of the first quarter of the 10th century AD. We know about her mostly from the literature of Rajasekhar, namely, the *Kavyamimamsa* – a treatise on poetics; dramas – the *Karpuramanjari* in Prakrit, *Balaramayana*, *Balabharat* in Sanskrit, and *Haravilasa*, an epic poem.

The name *Avantisundari* suggests that she was from the city Avanti. Her husband was apparently Maharashtrian by origin. In his drama *Balaramayana*, he writes that he is the fourth from *'Maharashtrachudamani Akaljalad'*.[1] It is well established that Rajasekhar lived in Maharashtra, especially in Vidarbha and adjacent provinces, namely Latdesh, Kuntal, etc. till his middle age.

From *Karpuramanjari*'s introduction, we know that Avanti was Rajasekhar's wife. She was from the Chauhan family.[2] The terms used to describe her suggest that she was a *'Kshatriyakanya'* married to the Brahman Rajasekhar according to the *anuloma* marriage system.

Avantisundari's Love for Prakrit

Avanti was not only a *Sanskritpandita*, but there are many proofs of her being a lover of Prakrit. For example, Rajasekhar's Prakrit drama, Karpuramanjari, was staged for the first time at the insistence of his wife Avantisundari.[3] She was also a great scholar of Prakrit, and it can be inferred that she wrote a treatise on Prakrit. The Jain poetician Hemachandra, who followed her two centuries later (12th century AD), quoted three Prakrit verses of Avanti in his treatise *Deshinamamala*.[4] Hemachandra also mentions new meanings of words which Avanti had given.

Avantisundari's Love for Literature

In Rajasekhar's *Kavyamimamsa*, we see that many times she expressed her views on serious and important topics of literature. For example, regarding *'Kavyapak'* – *'Paripakvata* of poetry' – she opposes the opinion of the disciples of Vamana, which gave importance to *'Shabdapak'*, and says that in poetry the words alone are not important. So the poet should not try for *shabdapak*, for it is *'vakyapak'* – *Paripakvata* of sentences – which is necessary in poetry. For that, the poet should select all the elements in poetry – the *alankar, riti, shabdarth,* etc. – suitable to the *rasa*. Only then does the poetry become *aasvadhya* or relishable.[5]

Rajasekhar appreciates this in a famous stanza –

"Sati vaktari satyarthe shabde sati rase sati

Asti tanna vina yen parisravati vangamadhu.

'Pak' is that factor without which *vangamadhu* does not flow in spite of the existence of all the elements like the poet (the speaker), meaning, words, *rasa* (sentiments), etc.[6]

In discussions on the selection of the subject of poetry, she said that in poetry the nature of a thing was not certain. Anything in itself was not *sarasa* or *nirasa*, but depended upon how the poet presented the thing.[7] If the poet were clever enough, he could describe the same thing differently in various enough, he could describe the same thing differently in various contexts. He could, for example, praise the moon as '*amrutansha*' (with rays full of nectar) in the context of one who is in the company of his beloved, and can castigate the same moon as '*donakar*' (a mine of faults) in the context of one separated from his beloved. So, according to her, anything could be the subject of poetry, for it was the treatment of the subject that was the distinguishing mark of a poet.

About plagiarism, too, her thoughts proved her shrewdness. While discussing plagiarism, Rajasekhar had stated that if plagiarism was natural and inevitable to a certain extent, then it was an art rather than a crime, and it was the poetician's duty to advice how to do it skillfully. To justify this he quoted the thoughts of Avantisundari, who guided the poets as follows:

"Ayamprasiddha prasiddhimanaham, ayampratishtha prathishthavanaham, aprakarantamidamasya samvidhankam orakrantam mama, guduchivachatodayam mrutvikavachano ham, anadritbhshavishesho yamahamahatbhasha–vishesha, prashantagyatrukaminda, deshantaritakartrukamidam, uccha (tsa)nanibandhanmulamind, mlecchikopanibandhanmulaminda mityevamadibhi karane shabdaharane arthaharane vabhirameta –ityavantisundari".[8]

In this passage, she advised poets to consider the following things before borrowing words and ideas from other poets:

(i) "I am famous; another one is not renowned."

(ii) "I have a status in society, while the other one has not."

(iii) "I am a well known dramatist, while the themes used by the other are not known to the public."

(iv) "I used a very refined language for expression of the content which has been expressed in a very rough manner by the other one."

(v) "I use the language which is very popular and respected by the people, while the other one uses language which is not much known.

(vi) One should make use of works which (a) are not known to many people *now*; (b) have been created by the authors of other countries; (c) whose basic roots are not available, and (d) which have been written in (not very prestigious) language.

It is not possible to discuss each and every way that she has suggested, but from the various possibilities that she has outlined for poets, it is clear that Avantisundari thought deeply about literature, and the skills to be used to make one's work better and more appreciated. The fact that Rajasekhar quoted her opinions with admiration, and did not record any objection to them, makes it clear that he fully agreed with her. It is also clear that others agreed with her, for Hemachandra also quotes this passage approvingly in his treatise, *Kavyanushasan*.

Regarding the family of the poet, Rajasekhar writes "*Prakritasanskrita bhashavida antapurika*" – the wives of poets should know both Prakrit and Sanskrit. Most probably, this statement is based on his own experience, for his wife Avantisundari was well versed in both languages, and knew what was good and bad. She must have appreciated his dramas and poetry, and evaluated them as they were. It obviously benefited his own creativity, hence the above suggestion.

It can be concluded from the above that Avantisundari was a lover of literature, lover of many languages, and she must have participated in the discussions in the '*kavigoshti*' (gathering of poets) along with her husband and other poets, and presented her views and opinions regarding various subjects confidently.

In conclusion, it appears that at least among the higher classes and the artistic and creative circles, women were given the opportunity to develop and express themselves in their own medium.

References

1. Shastri (ed.) - *Balaramayana, Rajasekhar*, p. 9.
2. Durgaprasad (ed.) – *Karpuramanjari*, p. 10
3. *Tattraiva*, p. 10

4. Bannerjee (ed.) – *Hemachandra – Deshinamamala* – (a) Verse 63, p. 29; (b) Verse 125, p. 52; (c) Verse 126, p. 52.
5. Dalal (ed.) – *Kavyamimamsa*, p. 20.
6. *Tattraiva*, p. 20.
7. *Ibid.*, p. 46.
8. *Ibid.*, p. 57.

6

Sati: An Epigraphic Perspective on Medieval Gujarat

By- Mrinal Joshi

The custom which was widely prevalent in medieval India and which affected the lives of women in the worst possible way was the custom of *sati*, that is burning alive of the widows with their deceased husbands. A lot of literature is available on *sati* and one may wonder, where is the need for yet another paper on the topic. It is true that most of the literary sources have been tapped for this purpose and to some extent the epigraphic sources have also been used for this purpose. However, we feel that epigraphic sources have not been fully utilized. This paper intends to make use of these sources.

Importance of epigraphy as a source of writing history can hardly be over-emphasized. Apart from the various other advantages of this source, it also highlights the regional peculiarities. The region we are concerned with, in this paper, is Gujarat. Gujarat is very rich in epigraphic records. Bibliography of the inscriptions of Gujarat published by the Gujarat Itihas Parishad, in several parts, during 1962-72, enlists 5,868 inscriptions.[1] If we add to this the inscriptions discovered and published in the subsequent period, the number may go up considerably. These inscriptions include those engraved on behalf of the rulers as well as those engraved on behalf of private individuals or organizations. We also come across another kind of inscription in Gujarat called *palias* or memorial stones. The number of such memorial stones located in Gujarat must be in thousands. Most of them date from 13th century C.E. to 18th century C.E. Out of these only few have been published. The published *palia* inscriptions consist approximately of hundred inscriptions engraved on the memorial stones of warriors and twenty on the memorial stones of *satis*.[2]

Epigraphic records have been a very valuable source of information for the political and cultural history of Gujarat. Right from A.K. Forbes and Bhagvanlal Indraji, almost all historians have availed themselves of this valuable source, especially for the ancient period. While discussing the epigraphical studies in Gujarat, one cannot but mention the name of H.D. Sankalia, who has enriched this field immensely. Two of his many important works are, *The Archaeology of Gujarat*[3] and *The Studies in Historical and Cultural Geography and Ethnography of Gujarat*[4]. The eminent epigraphist, H.G. Shastri has written several books on various aspects of Gujarat. One of his books, *The Historical and Cultural study of the inscriptions of Gujarat*[5] is based only on inscriptions. This paper intends to analyze the inscriptions on the memorial stones or *palias*, particularly of *satis* from the gender perspective.

The memorial stones bear inscriptions commemorating the demise of a person. Though most of these stones are erected in the memory of warriors or *satis*, they are also erected for the persons who laid their lives for other causes or even for those who died a natural death. The warriors were not always those who died in some war, but were also those who died while protecting the village, cows, Brahmins or women and children.

In the past, custom of religious suicide was also prevalent, like taking a fatal jump in the fulfilment of vows either for temporal or future good.[6] Another kind of religious suicide was called *Kamala-puja*. The person concerned would cut off his head in front of Lord Shiva as an offering.[7]

Yet another reason to sacrifice one's life was, as a protest against injustice. Some men and women performed self-immolation as protest against injustice. This was called *'traga'* in Gujarati. Such men and women usually came from *Carana* or Brahmin communities.[8]

Women burning themselves alive after the death of their husbands were referred to as *satis*. But there were a few cases when women as well as men sacrificed their lives after the death of a son, (in one case) daughter or some other relative.[9] They were also referred to as *satis* and *sats* (masculine form of *satis*). Nagji Bhatti informs us that there was even a case where a man, Charana Vala Bhoja, became *sat* after the death of his wife Venu, in V.S. 1727. This incident took place in Kachchh.[10] The author has not cited the inscription. We are unable to say whether the inscription has been published elsewhere or not. But the record is very important because of its uniqueness. If there were thousands of women who sacrificed their lives for their husbands, there was at least one man (could have been a few more also) who gave up his life after the death of his wife.

The purpose of giving various reasons for the self-sacrifice of men and women is to have an understanding about the values cherished by the people of medieval Gujarat. In this paper we are mostly concerned with the inscriptions on the memorial stones of *satis*. However, we have also utilized some records on the memorial stones of the martyrs in order to have a comparative perspective. Some literature on the memorial stones of Gujarat has been published, especially in Gujarati journals like *'Pathik* 'and *'Urminavarachana'*. The latter had taken out special issues on these *palias* in the year 1975. In these issues, authors like Nagji Bhatti, Hariprasad Shastri and others have contributed their articles. However, we have not yet come across the study of the inscriptions on the memorial stones of Gujarat from the gender perspective. No doubt, K.K. Shah in his paper, "Structural Approach to the Study of Inscriptions: Reinterpreting the Earliest Record of Self-immolation by a Widow", [11] has reinterpreted the 'Eran Stone Pillar Inscription of the year 510-11 C.E.' from the gender perspective, but the record is located in Madhya Pradesh.

For the past few years scholars have been expressing the need to make use of gender as a category of historical analysis. The inscriptions on the memorial stones can be effectively used for this purpose.

Practice of *sati* is the culmination of the values held by the people. These values are not absolute. They change not only according to time and space but also according to class, caste, religion and even gender. The present paper intends to analyze the *sati* inscriptions along the dimensions of caste, religion and gender.

We have been able to collect twenty inscriptions of *sati* from Gujarat, among which eleven are from Saurashtra, six are from Kachchh, two are from Bharuch and one is from Ahmedabad. Most of the records belong to the 17th century C.E. Four belong to the 14th c, two to the 18th c. and one each to 15th and 16th centuries. (Refer to Table 1) Below we are offering the summarized contents of these inscriptions.

1. This record tells us that in the year 1379 V.S. a woman named Chapade, who was the daughter of Nadeva and the wife of minister Prithvideva, became a *sati*. This record is from a place called Dumkal in district Bharuch. (HIG IV, inscription No. 103).[12]
2. The wording of this record is not clear, but it narrates the events of the death of Rana Shri Pratapasingh of Dumkal and committing of *sati* by his wife in the year 1443 V.S. (HIG IV, inscription No. 104)
3. The record mentions that on Friday, the first of the bright half of Phalguna, in V.S. 1448, a woman named Nayaki, mother of Patasi, became a *sati*. Patasi was the son of Samanta. The find spot of the record is Bagsara, district Junagadh. (I.K., April 1939, No. 51)
4. The inscription is from Chorwad, district Junagadh .The year of the record is V.S. 1450. It narrates the event of the death of Pathaka, of the Chudasama family, in a war. It also mentions that his wife Patasi become a *sati*. The

record is long and most part of this record describes the heroism of Pathaka, while the event of *sati* has been wrapped up in one line. (HIG IV, inscription no. 64)

5. This is a long record running into seventeen lines. It tells us about the donation by Sahadeva, of Tank caste (Rajput), for the construction of a step-well inV.S.1466. The donation was meant for the spiritual merit of his son Ashachandra, who had left this world. The last line of the record mentions that two women become *sati*. The names of the women or the name of their husband have not been given. But it seems that wives of Sahadeva become *satis* after the death of Sahadeva. Probably the line has been added after the death of Sahadeva. It has also been mentioned in the end that becoming *sati* is like a ladder to heaven. This record is from Dholka in district Bhavnagar. (HIG IV, inscription no. 7)

6. The inscription consists of two records of the year 1604 V.S. engraved on the same slab. One tells us about the death of Vaghela Vakta, son of Vaghela Hibamala, of Bagsara (Junagadh) while protecting the cows. The other record tells us that his wife Amena, daughter of Kancha Parvat and his wife Bai Ravi, became *sati*.
(HIG IV inscription no. 35-36)

7. This is the only Jaina *sati* record which we have come across. It is located at Ahmedabad. Rupchand, son of Sonpala and grandson of Rshabhadas died in 1672 V.S. Thereupon his three wives, Rupashri, Koma and Kesarajani burnt themselves on his funeral pyre.
(HIG IV, inscription no. 31)

8. This record which is from Varteja near Bhavnagar, records the event of committing sati by a Brahmin woman. In V.S.1674, a woman (name lost) of Kandoliya Brahmin caste became a *sati*. Rawal Dhunaji granted a sum of rupees for raising a memorial stone and a *deri* over it in honor of the lady. (HIG IV, inscription no. 145)

9. In V.S. 1674, a man named Kahana, who was the son of Bhaya and grandson of Dahi Samanta, died. His wife

Satimata became a *sati*. She was the daughter of Padaria Arjan. The find spot of this record is Gedi, district Kachchh.

(HIG V, inscription no. 150)

10. The record of the year V.S. 1677, which is located at a village called Mathak of Saurashtra, tells us that Bhojaraja, the son of Maharana Chandrasenji and his wife Paramara Bai Shri (sic.) Bhagavanta, left for heavenly abode. His wife Chavadi Bai shri (sic.) Vahala Bai became a *sati*. (HIG V, inscription no. 126)

11. This inscription from Vankaner in Rajkot district also belongs to Maharana Chandrasenji's family. It mentions that grandson of Chandrasenji, Shri Sartanji died in V.S. 1679. Thereupon his wife Rathod Shri (sic.) Pranavatibai became a *sati*. She was the granddaughter of Rai Shri Narayandasji of Idar and daughter of Kalyanamalji. The record further adds that Pranavati bai has gone to heaven along with Mahakuvar Sartanji.

(HIG V, inscription no. 132)

12. This record of V.S.1686, mentions the fact that Bai Harsha became a *sati*. Her father's name is mentioned but is not clear. Husband's name has not been given. The find spot of this record is village Gedi, district Kachchh.

(HIG V, inscription no. 152)

13. This inscription, which is located at Dahisara in district Rajkot, tells us that Bai Rudi, whose father was Mahanta Sahani, became a *sati* in V.S.1688. Her son raised a *deri* in her honour. The name of Rudibai's husband was Avadi Alodha, year of this record is V.S.1688.

(HIG V, inscription no. 85)

14. This inscription is knows as *Rathod ma no palio* or the memorial stone of Rathod mother, is yet another record of the family of Maharana Chandrasenji. It records the death of his grandson Shri Rajoji in V.S. 1699 and the subsequent event of becoming *sati* by his wife Shri (sic.) Ramkuvar. She was the daughter of Rathod Shri Iswardasji and his wife Bai Harshabai. The inscription is

located at Wadhawan in district Surendranagar.

(HIG V, inscription no. 134)

15. This record of V.S. 1688 records the death of Rau Shri Bharmallaji, son of Rau Shri Shengarji in Bhuj and becoming of *sati* by his wife Bai Lilavati in Bhuj. She was the daughter of Rao Mandalika of Chudasama family. Here ends the Gujarati portion. Then a Sanskrit verse is added in praise of Bharamallaji. Then again a Gujarati sentence is given, which tells us that a memorial was constructed by Raushri Tamchiji.

(HIG V, inscription no. 87)

16. This record mentions the death of Joshi Savaji, a Saraswat Brahmin, in V.S.1728. He was the son of Saraswat Joshi Harji and his wife Bai Raji. Bai Sarbai, wife of Savaji became a *sati* in Bhuj. She was the daughter of Joshi Somji and his wife Bai Vala. The record further adds that Bai Sarbai would go to heaven. (Urmi, p. 324)

17. In V.S. 1749, Gugali Brahmin woman named Ladbai became *sati* at the death of her husband Shankar Raghunath, who had performed *Kamala Puja*. The inscription is located at Khambalia in district Jamnagar.

(I.K. inscription no.15)

18 The record from Bhuj in Kachchh gives two dates, V.S. 1718 and V.S. 1776. First it says that in 1718 Bai Devaki became a *sati*. Next it mentions that another woman became a *sati* in 1776. However, who became *sati* in 1776 is not clear. (HIG V, inscription no. 95)

19. In V.S. 1797, Bai Devkuvar became a *sati* along with her husband Maharana Arjansinghji. She was the daughter of Amarasingji. In her honour, Parmara Maharana shri Sabalasinghji got constructed a *Prasada* or a temple. The record is located at Wadhwan in district Surendranagar.

(HIG V, inscription no. 135)

20. In V.S 1820 Thakar Shri Godho died and when his wife Malabai became *sati* a *deri* was raised in her honour. This record is from Bhuj. (Urmi, p. 324)

In most of our records the words used to indicate self-immolation are, sahagaman, *sagvan, sargaman* etc. In two inscriptions we come across the word *sati.* Out of these two one belongs to 15th century while the other to the 18th century. In one record we find Gujarati term *mat kidhu* being used. In the past, the act of self-immolation was performed in two ways. Generally widows burnt themselves along with the corpse of their husbands. This was known as *'Sahagamana'* or *'Sahamarana'*. If the husband died at a distant place from his wife, say in a battlefield and was cremated earlier, the widow burnt herself without the husband's dead body. This was known as *'Anumarana or 'Anugamana'*;[13] however in our records we have not come across the term *Anumarana.*

Analysis from Gender Perspective

As is evident from the inscriptions on the memorial stones, ideals laid down for men and women were different. Death on the battlefield for men, especially of warrior class, was highly valued. It was valued even more than the life itself. Similarly laying down one's life while doing one's duty such as protecting the village or cows from the enemies was also valued greatly. *Bhakti* or devotion to God was yet another ideal valued by the people. The acts like *kamlapuja*, mentioned above, were the extreme form of devotion. The men who lived up to these ideals were greatly respected by the society and it was believed that death for a just cause would take them to heaven.

The women were expected to be *pativratas* that is, fully devoted to their husbands, their lords. The practice of *sati* was the extreme point of this ideal. It was believed that a woman who burnt herself on the pyre of her husband, lived happily in heaven with her husband. Many women must have believed the statement that becoming a *sati* was a ladder to heaven.[14] For them the desire of a happy life with their husbands in heaven was as realistic as the desire to live happily with their husbands in this world. Thus, probably many women must have willingly chosen to die as *sati.* Of course there must have been cases of forced *sati* as well, but the number of women willingly embracing death after the death of their husbands must not have been less.

Men and women were indoctrinated into these values; however, in a patriarchal society more restrictions were put on women. Life for them was tougher than that for men. Men and women cherished these values and many sacrificed their lives for them. By laying down life for a 'just cause 'men and women not only earned merit for themselves, but also brought honour to their families.

The records 4, 6 & 17 are such records where both, husbands as well as wives have laid their lives for the ideals valued by them.

In (4) we find that Pathaka, died in the battlefield and his wife Patasi became a *sati.* Though both of them died for their ideals, the man has been eulogized while the woman has received very little epigraphic space. Here the andocentric bias of the composer is visible. K.K Shah made similar observation while analyzing the "Eran Stone Pillar Inscription of Bhanugupta".[15]

In (6) however, the case is different. This record also tells us that while the husband Vakta died while protecting the cows, his wife Amena became a *sati.* For both of these acts two separate records have been created. The contents of both the records are similar. If the father and grandfather of Vakta are mentioned, the parents of Amena also find mention. The sacrifices of both of them have been equally honoured.

In (17) we note that Joshi Raghunatha of Gugali Brahmin caste performed *kamala-puja* to Lord Shiva, that is gave his head as an offering to Lord Shiva. His wife, Ladbai, became a *sati.* A couple of lines each have been devoted to both of these events. Sacrifice of Raghkunatha and Ladbai both have been given equal weightage.

The inscription numbers 1, 2, 7, 9, 10, 11, 13, 14, 15, 16, 19, & 20 all are such records which indicate that the husbands have died a natural death and their wives have become *satis.* The inscriptions first mention the fact of the men's death and then the consequential event of their wives becoming *satis.*

Out of these, 7 and 15, are such records where in spite of the fact that husbands died natural death and their wives died for the ideal, husbands get more space. (7) is the only Jaina record of *sati*. It seems that father and uncle of the deceased man Rupchand, were rich and famous and were ministers in the court of Mughal emperor Jahangir.[16] The lineage of Rupchand is given. Three wives of Rupchand, who became *satis* are mentioned by their personal name alone. No other information about these women is given. While in (15), though the name of Bai Lilavati's father has been mentioned, more space has been accorded to Bharmallaji, her husband. In both of these records the andocentric bias of the composer or of the persons who provided the details of the record is visible. In the rest of the records women's sacrifice gets fair treatment. We also find *deris* being raised in honour of a couple of these women.

The inscription numbers 3, 8, 12, & 18 are such inscriptions, which mainly record the event of *sati*. In these records the husbands either do not find mention or even if mentioned are not the central figures. Inscription (3) records the event of Nayaki's (mother of Patasi) becoming *sati*. Probably Patasi was the engraver of this record. Nayaki's husband finds mention but only as the attribute of Patasi's identity and not as the attribute of her identity. Inscription number (8) is mutilated at certain places. The name of the Brahmin woman who become a *sati* is lost and her husband's name does not find mention. However, Rawal Dunaji, who raised a memorial stone and a *deri* in her honour is mentioned. In all probabilities he was the one who got the record engraved. Rawal Dhunaji came from Gohel family and thus probably was a Rajput.[17]

Inscription (12) mentions the fact of Bai Harsha's becoming a *sati*, while in inscription (18) the event of Devaki's becoming *sati* has been mentioned. In both of these records husbands do not find mention.

From the above analysis we note that, in most of the records, barring a few exceptions, sacrifice of women has got a fair treatment. If we compare these sati inscriptions with the inscriptions on the *palias* of men dying for a cause the point will become clear.

As noted above, most *sati* inscriptions mention the event of the husband's death and then the consequential event of the wife's becoming a *sati* is given. Names of her parents / father etc. are also generally given. The pattern of martyr's inscriptions is very much similar to this. They too are brief. They give the date of the event and then mention the event of the death of the hero in war or any such event.. Generally the names of hero's parents /father/ lineage is given. Sometimes the reigning king also finds mention. Below we give the summarized contents of a few of them.

1. It records the death, in a fight, of Pithia Anasa, son of Pithia Vasanga, at Nagichana in V.S. 1590.

   (I.K. 97)

2. It records the death in a fight while protecting the cows of Zala Bhimji, son of Gopalaji, son of Suryaji son of Lakhaji in V.S. 1687. (I.K. 128)

3. It records the death of Kathi Suma in a fight with the Mohammedan (Kabuli) Ayakhan in V.S. 1688.

   (I.K. 130)

Thus we can say that, as far as is evident from our records, the sacrifice of women becoming *satis* was as much valued as the sacrifice of men laying down their lives for their country, villages or any other purpose. Our aim here is not to eulogize *sati*. It is not to say that practice of *sati* was desirable. It was certainly an undesirable and cruel custom. The point here is that when it was accepted as an ideal to be cherished by the society, the women living up to this ideal were treated on par with the men who lived up to their ideals.

Analysis from Caste/Religious Perspective

If we consider the caste/ religion factor, we find that majority of the inscriptions mentioned above belong to the Rajputs. Three are Brahmin, one is Jaina and one belongs to Thakar caste. In a few inscriptions the caste is either not mentioned or is not clear. We have not come across any inscription of a *sati* from any of the Hindu Bania castes. This is clear from the table given below.

Sati Inscriptions of Gujarat – A Break-up

Century	*Region*				*Total no. of Inscriptions*	*Caste / Religion*			
	S	*K*	*N.G.*	*S.G.*		*R*	*B*	*O.H.*	*J*
14th	2	-	-	2	4	3	-	1	-
15th	1	-	-	-	1	1	-	-	-
16th	1	-	-	-	1	1	-	-	-
17th	6	5	1	-	12	5	3	3	1
18th	1	1	-	-	2	1	-	1	-
Total	11	6	1	2	20	11	3	5	1

S: Saurashtra, **R**: Rajput, **K**: Kachchh, **B**: Brahmin, **N.G.**: North Gujarat, **J**: Jaina, **S.G**: South Gujarat, **O.H**: Other Hindu castes. Of these one is Thakar.In other cases the caste is not clear.

The Rajput castes finding mention in our records are - Vaghela, Tank, Chudasama, Gohil, Parmar, Zala and Rathod. Our findings only confirm the oft-repeated statement that the practice of *sati* was more popular among the Rajputs.

The Brahmin castes finding mention in our records are– Kandolia, Gugali and Saraswat Joshi. However, Nagji Bhatti in his study of the *palias* of Kachchh,[18] has found the mention of other Brahmin castes such as Audichya, Trivedi, Pushkarni, Ojha–Brahmin, Nandavana, Pandya, Vyas and others. He has also found *sati* stones belonging to the other castes such as Carana-Gadhavi, Kayastha, Maheshwari, Lohana–Thakkar, Koli and others. However he has noted only one memorial stone of *sati* belonging to the Merchant caste, Modha. In the past people of this caste followed Jaina religion. But after the 18th century many of them got converted to Vaishnavism.[19] Nagji Bhatti has not cited this inscription, therefore it is very difficult to say whether the woman concerned was a Hindu or a Jaina.

Thus it becomes clear that practice of *sati* was valued by many Hindu castes. It was more prevalent among the Rajputs.

Cases of Brahmin *satis* may also have been quite considerable. But financing of the erecting of memorial stone may not have been possible for many Brahmins. In one case it seems that Rawal Dhunaji financed the memorial and *deri* in honour of a Brahmin lady.

The merchant castes consisted of Hindus as well as Jainas. Therefore it is plausible that the Hindu *Banias* were influenced by the Jaina religion. The Jaina women, like their Hindu sisters were expected to be *pativratas*. The ideal of *Pativrata* was greatly valued by the Jainas also, but this ideal was not stretched so far as to support the practice of *sati*. Among the Jainas, like the Hindus, widows were not allowed to remarry, but were expected to lead a chaste life. Jaina widows many a time preferred to become nuns. The practice of *sati* was not supported by Jainas, for they believed that the spiritual program of women, just like that of men, depended upon their own efforts. Becoming *sati* could not liberate a woman or give her a place in heaven.

Hindu *Banias* staying in close contact with the Jaina *Banias* probably imbibed these ideals and that is perhaps the reason why we find hardly any records of *sati* from the merchant castes.

However the influence was not only one sided. The Jainas also, to some extent were influenced by the Hindu, especially Rajput values. The case of the Jaina *satis* which we have mentioned (illustration 7) is an example of this phenomenon. The Jaina *satis* came from Osval caste. Their family members were in the service of Mughals and therefore probably came in close contact with Rajputs. These women were thus more influenced by the Rajput values than the religious prescriptions of their own religion. They may have even been unaware of the prescriptions of their own religion. The other possibility is that the family members felt that the women of their family becoming *satis* would help in enhancing the prestige of their family. In that case the women may have been forced to become *satis*. This suggests that perhaps the cross-cultural influences affected the practice of *sati* among various castes and religions of Gujarat.

In a gendered society, the ideals that a man is expected to live up to are different from the ideals that a woman is expected to live up to. Most of the societies being patriarchal put more restrictions on women and women are subordinated to men. But the injustice does not end here. Many a time even when the women lived up to ideals set for them, they do not receive the same honour and respect, which a man in a similar position would receive. Gujarat society was also a patriarchal society. However, in our study of the *sati* inscriptions of Gujarat we find that in majority of the cases women living up to their ideals received the respect and honor which the men living up to the ideals received. We find *satis* being honoured in the similar way as the martyrs were. It may be that the intention behind thus honouring *satis* was to reconfirm and indoctrinate the values of *pativrata* and *sati* in the minds of the people. Or else it may be out of genuine respect for the *satis*.

Practice of *sati* is supposed to be a Hindu custom and therefore we expected to find cases of *satis* in all Hindu castes, though in different proportions. As the Jainas do not support the practice of *sati* we did not expect to find any instances of *sati* among the Jainas. However we could find one instance of *sati* among the Jainas and no case of *sati* among the Hindu *Banias*. This indicates that cross-cultural influences affected the practice of *sati* among various castes and religions of Gujarat.

References

1. *Gujarat Itihas Sandarbha Suchi*, Vol.–I to VI, Ahmedabad, Gujarat Itihas Parishad, 1962-72
2. Hariprasad Shastri, 'Khambi Paliya ane ena Abhilekh' in *Urminavarachana*, Nov. 1975, p.390.
3. H.D. Sankalia, *Archaeology of Gujarat*, Bombay, Natwarlal & Co., 1941.
4. ______, *Studies in the Historical & Cultural Geography and Ethnography of Gujarat: Places and People in the Inscriptions of Gujarat, 300 B.C.-1300 B.C.*, Poona, Deccan College P.G. and Research Institute, 1949.
5. H.G. Shastri, *A Historical and Cultural Study of the Inscriptions of Gujarat*, Ahmedabad, B.J. Institute of Learning and Research, 1989.

6. M.R. Majumdar, *Cultural History of Gujarat*, Bombay, Popular Prakashan, 1965, p.337.
7. Nagaji K. Bhatti, 'Paliyanu Sarvekshan ek Abhyas' in *Urminavarachana*, August 1975, p.222.
8. Nagji K. Bhatti, 'Kachchhna Khambi Palia ek Abhyas', in *Urminavarachana,* September 1975, p. 320
9. Jayamalla Paramar, 'Khambi ne Paliya Abhyas na Kshetrama', in *Urminavarachana,* November, 1975, p. 366.
10. Ibid.
11. K.K. Shah, 'Structural Approach to the Study of Inscriptions: Reinterpreting the Earliest Record of Self-immolation by a Widow', in *S.N.D.T. Women's' University Research Journal,* Vol., XI.1999, p.76.
12. Abbreviations used in this paper-
    (i) HIG – Hariprasad Shastri, *Historical Inscriptions of Gujarat*, Forbes Gujarati Sabha, Bombay, Vol. IV-1979, Vol. V-1981.
    (ii) I.K.– D.R. Diskalkar, *Inscriptions of Kathiawar*, Karnataka Publishing House, Bombay, 1944.
    (iii) Urmi–*Urminavarachana,* Vol. 46, 1975-76.
13. Hariprasad Shastri, 'Khambi Paliya ane ena Abhilekh' *in Urmi,* Nov. 1975, p. 389.
14. *Supra* p.4, citation No. 5
15. K.K. Shah, *op.cit.*
16. HIG, P. 55.
17. IK, p. 281
18. Nagji K. Bhatti, 'Paliyanu Sarvekshan ek Abhyas', *Urmi*, August, 1975, p. 262.
19. Buddhisagar Suriji, *Jaina Dhatun Pratima Lekha Sangraha–I,* Mumbai, Shri Adhyatma Prasaraka Mandala, 1917, p. 16.

7

Women Journalism in Gujarati: A Study in Expression of Gender Perception (1850-1920)

Shirin Mehta\`

Gujarati women stepped forward as entrepreneurs of new enterprise in the field of journalism in the latter half of the nineteenth century. The women journalists, writers and women reformers instrumented popular literature as a media to disseminate their own sensitivity and perception about the things around. The reformers were equally interested in resculpturing women. As a result there was influx of women periodicals initiated by males as well as females around 1850. But unfortunately to investigate women's consciousness through popular writings, literature and journalism, Gujarat has remained a relatively neglected area of concern.

Initially, educated women belonging to upper strata of the society appeared as editors and contributed significantly not only in the field of journalism but also in the history of women's movement. Women like Tulsibai, Parvatikunvar, Jarbanu Dinshaw, Putalibai Kabarajee, Shirin Kabarajee, Sakina Abdulbhai, Vidyaben Nilkanth and Shardaben Mehta were the leading figures in the area of journalism. For instance, **Parhejgar** (a watchman that awakes) was started by Parhejgar Sabha in 1845. The well-known social reformer and littérateur

Mahipatram Ruparam was its editor. In fact, his wife Parvatikunvar ran the show. Right from the selection of articles, proof-reading and processing for postal delivery, everything was looked after by her.[1] Similarly, **Stribodh** and **Rashte Ghoftar** were floated by Parsi Ke Khushro Kabarajee, a zealous reformer, but after his death in 1881 they were taken over by his daughter Shirin and daughter-in-law Putalibai. Both were trained by Kabarajee. This group of journalists also included women from remote far-flung areas of Gujarat.[2] For instance, Tulsibai, who belonged to village Kheda in central Gujarat issued a journal **Stri-Bodh Ratna** in 1882.[3] These women editors and writers might be 'minor' in their total output but as a group they provide us with a clear sense of what women were thinking and writing about. The contemporary women journals comprehensively dealt with almost all aspects that touched women's lives. All over the country women had hardly begun to read and write and yet some women became editors and writers.

The entrance of women in the field of journalism as a new venture in 1850s raised some issues which require to be debated and discussed. Was women's perception as expressed in journals was different from that of men? Or did she toe the male line alone? Since social reform movement was the most pervading phenomena in the selection process, which were the aspects that perturbed women most? What was the nature of women's consciousness, did they view women's issues in terms of ethnic diversity, in class or in gender category? And, finally, was there any change over a period in the style of writing, the themes they covered or the tone or ideology that they focussed on, or the types of clientele?

To answer these questions the paper is divided into three parts. Each part marks a turning point constituting a watershed of development according to historical forces in the field of journalism. The first phase of Women's journalism began from 1850 to 1880. The second phase covered the period 1880-1900 and the last from 1900 to 1920 encompassed the period before Gandhian era.

I

Thematic Contours of Earlier Phase of Journalism

The first phase of journalism was marked by Euro-centric writings having positive, supportive appraisal of British rule. The magazines highlighted European culture, science and technological innovations: so much so that they prescribed 'Victorian English Women' as the model to be imitated by Gujarati women. Secondly, the Social reform movement secured wide coverage in mass media and finally, only upper class woman was identified in the journals. 'Aryan-Woman' was redefined in the new set up congruent with the 'Victorian-Woman' icon.[4]

Why did the earlier phase of women's journalism centre around the parameters of European Civilisation?

The delineation of themes consciously or unconsciously had been prescribed by the colonial masters. The British conquest established not only power domination by force but cultural superiority by consent. The tactical manoeuvring of ideological domination of racism upholding the white norms as standard was uncannily associated with accurate historical process. "We are the dominant race" they popularised the phrase. They subtly introduced it through English education as infra-structural measure. The hegemonic imposition of European culture was the mainstay of discourse between the colonials and the colonised.[5]

Women became a crucial component in the imperialists' discourse. The British with better civilizing claim of liberalism, equality and democracy kept the floodgates of criticism wide open on the issues of women. They levelled serious onslaughts on barbaric practices like Sati, female infanticide, child marriage, dowry, low status of women, plight of widows etc.

The English–educated intelligentsia were baffled and perplexed at the instance of cross-cultural currents. The assault on their culture touched their very core. Wounded as they were, experiencing inferiority–complex as defeated nation, they embarked upon the programme of social reforms for the moral transformation of a perverse society. They gave angularity to women, advocated female education, widow remarriage, ban on sati, female infanticide, child marriage, dowry etc.[6]

But the encounter of the colonised with the colonial was ambiguous, and ambivalent. To overcome colonial domination they realised the importance of science, technology, modernity, liberalism and democracy that had brought large areas of the world under European domination. But they could not reconcile this with the deeply ingrained traditional structures of caste, patriarchy and religious scriptures. They preferred to compartmentalise their lives. Outside home they preferred to be western and modern but at home they lived to maintain Indian culture, religion, rituals and traditional forms. Women so far were confined to home and hearth and became increasingly identified as the carriers of tradition, custodians of religion and torchbearers of Indian culture. The **'Aryan-Kshatriya Woman'** as ideal or **'Gruha-Priya Devanagana'** model (home loving divine angel) was entirely suitable for this task.

In the beginning the women oriented journals concentrated on upper class woman, for the writers and readers belonged to the same segment. Hence the concept of 'Aryan womanhood' was elitist in terms of class and caste. The **Bhadra mahila** – elite woman, became paradigmatic in literature and journals. Along with this image was historically associated the woman of Victorian age, the construction of which was entirely in consonance with **Aryan – Kshatriya woman**.[7]

Victorian ideals centred on the English Woman. She should glory in her womanliness, god-given weakness, tenderness, and feminine charm. Nature had prescribed reciprocity of abilities between men and women. She should maintain domesticity, family life and companionship to man. The acceptance of these values in a way became sub-culture of the colonised. It was deemed remarkable to undergo this feat of reculturization by women.[8]

The Ideological Framework Illustrated through Journals

Stri Bodh

The Parsis in Gujarat were pioneers in the field of women journalism. Though they were conscious of their ethnic diversity since they hailed from **Persia** and followed **Zoroastrian** religion, they existed as a subsect of the total composite culture of Gujarat. The Parsi Gujarati was typically full of humourous style. The Parsis' dramas were the most popular form of literature in Gujarati. They were a highly Westernised community in India, and were the first to take up English education for their girls.[9]

Stri Bodh, set up in 1857, by the Bombay-based group of Parsi Social reformers like Behramjee Gandhi, Sorabjee Shahpurjee Bengali etc., was the first woman's journal in Gujarati. Ke Khushro Kabarajee was its editor. It was sheer coincidence that the year in which **Stri Bodh** saw the light of the day was followed by a parallel event - the rebellion of 1857. Maintaining a pro-British stance, it stigmatized the rebellers as "enemy miscreants revolting against 'our government".[10]

The objective of **Stri-Bodh** was to propagate English education and to Westernise and modernise Parsi women. Parsi women were equally intent upon proving their ability to attain intellectual calibre and strength of character on par with that of white women. The educated Parsi women provided proof through their writings in journals that they had assimilated the culture of the occupying power.

On the very title page there appeared a saying under the name of Napoleon. It read, "Napoleon said the best way to prosper the nation was to educate women" (*Kane Napoleon Deshne Larva Abadan do mata ne Gyan*). The journal consisted of exotic English tales, romantic narratives of adventurous feats of Europeans, their works, history, poems, scientific innovations, discoveries etc. It also presented exhaustive profile of European women like Joan of Arc, Florence Nightingale, Mary Carpenter, Margaret Cousin and the wives of British bureaucrats. More and more articles appeared on health and hygiene, child caring and rearing, how to pass leisure time, how to maintain youthfulness. In a nutshell, the presentation of the image of Victorian woman was a salient feature of the journal.[11]

The three Parsi Women who played a leading role in shaping, moulding and developing the journal, were Putalibai Jahangir Kawasjee, the daughter-in-law if Ke Khushro, her mother Jarbai Dhanjeebhai Wadia and Shirin Kabarajee, Khushro's daughter. Shirin was unmarried and the journal was the mission of her life. Putalibai was matriculate in those days and she was very fond of English literature. Her husband was a collector and she was in constant touch with the Britishers. She undertook the task of translating, "Chamber's short stories". Her work drew the attention of Captain Tempelle, the editor of the periodical **Indian Antiquity**. Her interview was published in that magazine. Shirin simultaneously translated popular English literature in Gujarati. The story of Jekyll and Hyde, Shakespearean dramas, 'As You Like It' and 'King Lear' and a book of Lord Evberry, **The use of Life,** all these translations were regularly serialised in **Stri Bodh.**[12]

The Parsi promoters of the magazine soon realised a serious flaw since it was merely Parsi women-centric. To make it commercially viable they incorporated non-Parsi men of letters like Karsandas Mulji, Mangaldas Nathabhai, Nanabhai Haridas in the Board of Editors in 1868. They channellised the social reform movement through **Stri Bodh**. The articles advocating female education, removal of backward customs and many aspects touching women were written. But it continued to keep a moderate liberal stance. It did not join in the debates on contentious burning issues like Maharaj Libel case (1862), Phulmani Das case (1891), Age of Consent Bill (1891).

Stri-Mitra (1867) -Bombay

The Parsis continued to dominate Gujarati women journalism. **Stri-Mitra** on the same wavelength was introduced in 1867 by noted Parsi social reformers Rustamjee Ranina and a publisher of Bombay Union Press Rustamjee Pastanjee Vakil. Besides essays and notes on general topics like health, hygiene, female education, it concentrated on specific issues. It started discussing the cases of child marriage, dowry deaths, and violence on women. It criticised patriarchal norms for thirty years. But it was closed down in 1907.[13]

Gujarati Shala Patra - (1861), Ahmedabad

It was the first non-Parsi magazine. The monthly was promoted by the Education Department of the Government. Mahipatram Ruparam, the doyen of Gujarati literature was appointed as its editor. It projected well the traditional values of Indian culture to suit the general climate of the society.

The journal aimed to inculcate value-based education in girls right from the primary to high school. She should be a good daughter, caring wife, nursing mother and true companion of her husband. In short she was couched in 'Gruha Priya Devanagna' and 'Companionate' model. Being a pompous government enterprise the title page gave a heading with bold letters in praise of crown. It read,[14]

"The Queen Empress Victoria – the Grand
Title Holder, Kaiser-i-Hind-the Divine King,
Her Diamond Jubilee Festival – a Divine Garden".

Below that, a couplet glorifying woman was published,

"There is no home without woman
There is no citizen without Home
And no state without Citizen
There is no prosperity of nation without woman".

All the girls' schools run by the government were required in their prayers before the routine classes to sing a garba song titled. '*Strione Shikhamanano Garba*' (a garba song to advise girls). It was written by Mehtaji Vrajbhukhan Dalpatram of a Government School, **Godhavi in Saurashtra.** It was so widely circulated that it had four editions, each with reduced price. From four annas it was brought down to one anna. The girls were advised to be womanly, polite, enduring. She should serve her in-laws and above all her husband. She should never speak ill of him even if he abused her, shouted at her or was angry with her, for he was god incarnate for her.[15]

Thus the first phase of journalism remained Euro-centric. The social-reformers were selective in adopting liberalism, enlightenment, and scientific approach. Women were redefined as Sati, Sita, Savitri. Women of this age also actually underwent acculturation and tried to imitate Victorian woman who echoed their own cultural values.

II

Second Phase – 1880-1900

At the turn of the 19th century, a few changes in a more positive direction began to appear. Women acquired subjectivity and centrality. Women became conscious of their identity and gathered courage to be expressive, vocal and vociferous about their problems during the second stage of journalism between 1880-1900.

The most outstanding publication during this period was **Stri Gyan Deepak (1868).** It was not a weekly, fortnightly or monthly. This journal was started in 1868 but after 1880 it took a concrete shape. One Parsi teacher Sorabjee Mancherjee Bhagolia of Parsi English School, Gamdevi, Surat embarked on a new experiment to bring out a collection of good articles on women issues from different women journals in a concise form. He gave it the same name **Stri-gyan Deepak** – women's lamp of knowledge. It was a voluminous work, a compendium of select articles. Every year after 1880 it was published. It was Bhagolia's cherished desire that this volume must have a place on every woman's table.[16]

This volume had a discursive character. Articles written by women only were included. "Women and social Injustice", 'Female Education as the Panacea of all Evils', 'Dwi Striya Nishedh', 'Bahu-Patnitwa: the Root cause of Malaise'. Such articles reflected the level of consciousness being acquired by women.[17]

The most remarkable feature of this compendium was the section on widows encompassing an authentic revelation of their plights. Bhagolia was perturbed by the condition of Hindu widows, which touched the nadir of degradation of Hindu society. Bhagolia brought to the limelight stories of these distressed women told and written by them, though anonymously. Hardly any widow really seemed to accept remarriage as an alternative. Many widows had been forced into child-marriage into a Kulin family with on old man, which resulted in enforced widowhood. She was constantly to be the clear target of rape, sex abuse, voluptuous nature of men. The stories revealed the obverse side of the hypocritical, corrupt society of the nineteenth century.[18] In his endeavour, a Parsi reformer of note, Behramjee Malbari of Bombay (1853-1912) played a supportive role to Bhagolia. Malbari wrote an essay on "Notes on Infant Marriage and Enforced Widowhood" that created serious ripples throughout India in 1884. He pressurised the government to raise the marriageable age of a bride and bridegroom. Malbari did not limit his activity to merely writing an article on widows.[19] He brought out a sizeable book on **Gujarat and Gujaratis**. He gave wide platform to widows. His book presented various interesting abstracts on the life of widows. One Moghi Thakkarani's account was superb. She was courageous enough to mention her name. She boldly confessed her promiscuous relationship with the connivance of her husband and her in-laws. She described in detail how the head priest of the Vaishnav sect had seduced her, in opposition to and in spite of the judgement of the Maharaj Libel Case (1861).

At the end of 19th century the entertainment and informative aspect in journalism was replaced by more issue-based, problem-oriented writings. There was an influx of caste journals. Of course, they were not strictly women periodicals but women got a wide spectrum to express themselves. Caste journals like **Nagar Mitra** (1892), **Anavil Hitechhu** (1896, Surat), **Patidar Hitechhu** (1908, Baroda), **Patel Bandhu** (1908, Baroda), **Anavil Sevak** (1910, Surat) **Anavil Pokar** (1911, Surat), **Anavil Jagat** (1911, Surat) etc. actually launched campaigns to reform caste and to remove evil practices. But few reformers ever questioned the existence of the caste structure. They wanted to bring change within the framework of caste.[20]

In the caste journals women came out with different expressions of their internalised agony. They did not accept the imposed concocted agenda of social reforms. They wrote through their own experiences and realisations. For instance, Tara Desai wrote in **Anavil Hitechhu** (November 2, 1816, Vol.2), a poem on the victim of child marriage,[21] "Child-marriage: the Agony of an aggrieved woman". She described in the poem how her friends ridiculed her doll-spouse. She said in the end, "adultery abounds, submission of soul, mind and body all around, I ask painfully who was to end the evil?" There were some farcical, humourous poems also on the same topic. Navalram Mehta, a poet of Surat, wrote a satirical poem, "Advantages of the Child Marriage".

When Tulsibai from the remote village of Kheda in central Gujarat started a journal **Stri Sad Bodh Ratna** in October 1882 a new chapter was added in the history of women journals. Through this journal she entered into crusade against dowry, polygamy and endogamy, the most prevalent customs among Patidars and Anavil Castes of Kheda. This malaise was the outcome of the prosperous cash crop economy during the British rule.[22]

No woman writer during this phase opted for widow-remarriage. The Punar Vivah Uttejak Mandali and Widow Remarriage Act 1856 were big failures. The women leaders questioned the British government as to why should not government try to eliminate second marriage of a husband when first wife was alive. Jamnabai Pandita, a teacher in Jamnagar asked the government to put a ban on polygamy rather than to encourage widow remarriage. Another woman Gangabai Yagnik a principal of Mama Girls School wrote a book titled "Dwi Striya Nishedh".[23]

During the second stage of journalism Euro-centric and pro-British-rule stance was replaced by critical evaluation of colonial rule. The euphoria of Victorian woman and legitimacy of Aryan womanhood were effaced. The element of self-identity began to be visible in women's writings.

III

Last Phase - 1900-1920

With the advent of the twentieth century women's education became a more widespread phenomenon. There was a noticeable thematic change. The dry, drab, rhetoric, academic debates on female education, reforms were replaced by dynamic, vibrant, empirical data-based writings. A breakthrough resulted in the history of journalism when the lowest strata of women got visibility in the news. Tribal, scheduled caste women got subjectivity. During the first decade of the twentieth century journalism, women saw women in gender category – 'all women' were put in one 'umbrella' cutting across caste, class and community. The radius of the circulation of journals increased by leaps and bounds, they encompassed even the peripheral and rural areas. Journalism became in the true sense of the term real mass media. New types of journals were set up for the first time. Women's organisations issued their own journals as their mouthpieces. It was, in fact, the journey from **Bhadra Mahila** to **Bhil Mahila.**

Sundari Subodh - September 1903, Ahmedabad

A group of littérateurs in Ahmedabad like Mahipatram Ruparam, Krushnarao Bholanath Divetia, Rammohan Jashwantrao Desai, all were the protagonists of female education, equal status, social justice and women's rights. They found a dire need to start a journal exclusively for women. They appreciated **Stri Bodh** but found it Parsi-centric. Rammohan Desai was its editor. Under the auspices of **Bandhu Samaj** (Ahmedabad) a rationalist association started a magazine named **Sundari Subodh** in September 1903. In his first editorial, 'Stri Lekheo anne temni Shailli' (women writers and their style of writing) he gave a clarion call to all women writers "to step forward and to write fearlessly without thinking societal reactions". He encouraged women by expressing immense faith in their abilities.[24]

Sundari Subodh was a watershed in the history of women's journalism. "Woman", not the upper class **Bhadra Mahila,** but as a gender category was negotiated for the first time. The very first issue of the magazine published a poem entitled "The song of Bharati Women". It was a song of women of India expressing the cherished desire to come together to serve the nation. It stated,[25].

> 'The song of Bharati-Women'
>
> Gujarati, Bang-Sunderi together, Kashmiri, Dravidi, Maharashtri, Rajputani all
>
> Let us together sing song of unity,
>
> Parsi, Islami, Arya Ramanies (beauties) European
>
> Sannaries (gentle ladies) spirited, romantic
>
> and enthusiastic all of us
>
> Let us all together O! Sisters pray to Hind-Devi.

Shakinabibi Abdulbhai, a Khoja Muslim from Mudra, a port of Kutch, wrote many poems in praise of Allah, urging for peace and women's uplift. Shrimati Badrudin Lukmani, a Muslim woman, and Jarbanu Bharucha, a Parsi woman, were regular contributors. The December 1903 issue of Stri Bodh published the news of the founding of the Anjuman-i-Islam Muslim Girls School with much fanfare under the heading 'News of Great Happiness'.

The February 1908 issue of Sundari Subodh was a landmark. It gave wide coverage to Bhil Conference convened at Godhra. It reported in detail the various resolutions passed by Bhil Conference in favour of Bhil Women. The conference put a ban on the behaviour of the Bhil man. He could not marry a Bhil Woman whose husband was alive. He could not desert his wife on any grounds, and he had to maintain his wife it she got any physical disability after marriage. The report ended with the editorial remark, 'Even the Bhils now have exalted status of women'. The new experiment in the field of education department of the Baroda State was well covered in the August 1908, issue of the periodical. The education department celebrated 'Mothers' day', and invited mothers of girls from all schools of the state. The issue described that mothers from Koli, Kachhiya, Sutar, Kumbhar Kadiya – the lower castes - attended the festival and enjoyed themselves.[26]

The Journals as mouthpieces of women's organisations:

Women's organisations mushroomed with the coming of the twentieth century. Women's clubbing together for organising efforts in search of ideality was a significant stage in women's movement. Initially during 1880, they crystallised into a club similar to western style organisations. But with the lapse of the time there emerged organisations like **Bhagini Samaj** (Ahmedabad), **Hindu Stri Mandal** (1903, Ahmedabad), **Vanita Vishram,** (1907, Surat, 1915-Bombay, 1921-Rajkot, 1922 Bhavanagar). **Vanita Vishram** was also founded at Ahmedabad in 1907 by other founders. **Saraswati Mandir** (1906, Ahmedabad) also was established.

Organisations like **Hindu Stri Mandal** and **Vanita Vishram** with their widespread organisational networking found it worthwhile to start their own magazines to give expression to their inmates. **Hindu Stri Mandal** started its journal **Stri-Hitopadesh** in 1909. In the same year Vanita Vishram, Surat a central, nucleus organisation issued a journal **Vanita Vigyan.**[27]

Stri-Hitopadesh, 1909, Bombay

Befitting the composite culture of Gujarat, cross-sections of women were its contributors. The special Diwali issue asked all women to get united forgetting about their differences of creed, caste and class. It published the famous couplets[28] of Dindervesh, a Sufi poet of 16th century, cited below:

Hindu called him Superior; Muslim had the same utterance,

Both the two sides of the same coin,
who is greater, who is smaller,
Never to draw divider,
One devotee of Ram, the other of Rahim Se Raziya
God, one and only one, Superior to all.

The 'Amrutvani' section of **Stri-Hitopadesh** was very popular. The journal covered Gujarati Diaspora in East Africa, South Africa also. The news of the South Africa Satyagraha launched by Gandhiji frequently featured during the period 1908-1914. The objectives of **Stri-Hitopadesh,** besides propagating female education, were, service to humanity, vocational training to women across the threshold of the kitchen. When the arid and dry climate of Saurashtra and Kutch faced severe famine in 1911, the founder members Jamnabai Sakai, Putlibai Sethan, Janakibai Bhatt toured these regions for three months. They collected funds, distributed food, fodder and other necessities, moving from door to door. They channelised women's energy into meaningful directions. **Stri-Hitopadesh** launched a campaign at the time of the famine. Its wide reporting, heart rendering photographs of famine-stricken areas, dying cattle, heaps of bones made people conscious of the gravity of the situation.[29]

Stri-Hitopadesh produced a galaxy of women writers in Jamnabai Sakai, Vidyaben Nilkanth, Shardaben Mehta, Harisukhgauri Vamanrao, Krishnagauri Raval (the first woman novelist of Gujarat, her novel Sadguni Hemant Kumari became very famous), Vijyalaxmi Trivedi the poetess, Shrimati Baddrudin Lukamani etc.

Vanita Vigyan (1909, Surat) as a magazine was in fact the instrument to carry the objectives of **Vanita Vishram,** to a logical end. Vanita Vishram was an organisation established by two widows of Surat after a long spell of the their widowhood, Naniben or Shivagauri Gajjar (1871-1945) and Bajigauri Munshi (1866-1926). It was a mother's home for child-widows, deserted girls, and distressed women. Besides providing shelter it aimed of providing economic self-sufficiency for honourable living to widows. It wanted to break the age-old shackles of compartmentalisation of activities between man and woman. **Vanita Vishram** aspired to make woman a breadwinner.[30]

Vanita Vigyan was an effort to vocalise these goals. It published Bhajans and prayer songs to give solace to distressed girls. It inculcated moral, ethical values and religious orientation so that girls could psychologically adjust to the hardcore realities. **Vanita Vigyan** gave wide publicity to handicraft exhibitions, knitting and embroidery specimens and professional courses. It structured these as women's science. **Vanita Vigyan** was a journal of Ashramites. They wrote their own experiences, many times anonymously and praised the role of **Vanita Vishram** in developing their lives.[31]

One student wrote, "I got married into a Kulin family, I was beautiful. My husband had no capacity to earn. Both my husband and his mother wanted me to encash my beauty and encouraged me indirectly to earn as sex worker. I left home and ran away, joined **Vanita Vishram.** Now I am a teacher and earn my living with head held high".[32]

Another woman Tara Vakil was nostalgic when she described her very first day in Vanita Vishram. She told her story through **Vanita Vigyan,** in these words, "I was four years of age when I lost my mother. My father found it difficult to bring me up; he was helpless. He arrived at **Vanita Vishram** to entrust me to their care with tremendous faith. A white sari-clad woman came, she looked pious and warm. When my father pleaded my case, she with tender voice told my father 'the law of the organisation could not enter the child when one of the parents is alive'. My father requested her and stepped down went away leaving me behind. I cried and wept 'O mother, mom'. The woman in white took me in her lap, embraced me, consoled me and said 'I am your mother my child'. She was my mom, Naniben Gajjar!"[33] Thus it was a students' journal in right earnest.

Gulshan (1915, Navasari), **Saraswati** (1915, Bharuch) were popular journals with beautiful photographs and stories catering to the reading habits of the masses. **Gulshan** was floated by Dinshaw Bhagolia and **Saraswati** by Pareen Davar. Parsis continued to dominate Gujarati journalism.[34]

Gujarati journals fulfilled their task of making women conscious. When Gandhiji took up the leadership women were already mobilized and situation was already ripe. Gandhiji was required to sow the seeds, the ground was already fertile. Women were ready to be the significant cogs of his machinery to carry his constructive programme and non-violent movements.

References

1. Ratan Marshal, *Gujarati Patrakaritvano Itihas,* Surat, 1950, pp. 19-25.
2. *Gujarati Shala Patra,* Ahmedabad, Rajkot, 1871 Vol. VI, p. 69
3. Ibid; Vol IX, 1874, p. 15
4. Gauri Viswanathan, *Masks of Conquest; Literary Study and British Rule* London, 1991, pp. 1-17.
5. Kumkum Sangari and Sudesh Vaid (ed), *Recasting Women: Essays in Colonial History,* New Delhi, 1989 p. 8.
6. Maitrayee Chaudhari, *Indian Women's Movement: Reform and Revival* New Delhi, 1991, pp. 20-25.
7. Uma Chakravarti, *Rewriting History: The Life and Times of Pandita Ramabai,* New Delhi, 1998, pp. 56.
8. Patricia Hollis, *Women in Public, 1850-1900: Documents of Victorian Women's Movement,* London, 1979, p. 88.
9. Ratan Marshal, N. 1, p.16
10. Ibid; p. 53
11. *Stri Bodh,* Bombay January 1858, No. 2, Vol. 2, p. 6.
12. Ibid., April 1883, Bombay, No. 1, Vol. 27, p. 183.
13. *Stri Mitra,* (Bombay, September 1907) Vol. 7, No. 7, p. 14.
14. *Gujarati Shala Patra* (Ahmedabad, 1911) Vol. V, No. 3, p. 116.
15. Mehtaji Vrajabhukhan Dalpatram, *Striono Shikhaman No Garbo* Ahmedabad, 1869.
16. Sorabjee Mancherjee Bhagolia (ed); *Stri Gyan Deepak,* Bombay, 1868 Union Press, pp. 1-10.
17. Ibid. Bombay, 1881, Vol. 13, p. 54.
18. Ibid. Bombay, 1885 Vol. 17, p. 69.
19. Malbari Behramji M., *Infant Marriage and Enforced Widowhood,* Bombay, 1887, p.9.
20. B. M. Malbari, *Gujarat and Gujaratis,* Bombay, 1883, p. 85.

21. *Nagar Mitra* 1892; *Anavil Hitechhu*, Surat, 1896; Patidar Hitechhu, Baroda, 1908; *Patel Bandhu* Baroda, 1908; *Anavil Sevak,* Surat, 1910; *Anavil Jayat*, Surat, 1911.
22. *Anavil Hitechhu*, November 2, 1896, Vol. 2, p. 34.
23. *Buddhiprakash*, Ahmedabad, 1884, Vol. 30, p. 164.
24. Pandita Jamnabai, *Stri Dharma,* Jamnagar, 1891, p. 216; Gangabai Yagnik, *Dwi Striya Nishedh,* Mansa, 1892, p. 61.
25. Sundari Subodh, Bombay, September 1903, Vol. 1, p. 5.
26. Ibid. p. 9.
27. Ibid; December 1912, Vol. 9, p. 25, January 1913, Vol 10, p. 6; February 1913, Vol. 11, p. 15; March 1913, Vol. 12, p. 8.
28. Stri Hitopdesh, Bombay, 1909, Vol. 1, p. 1; Vanita Vigyan, *Vanita Vishram Prashashti Ank*, Surat, 1973 p. 5.
29. *Stri Hitopdesh: Jamnabai Sakkai Smarak Ank* Bombay, 1919, pp. 20-21.
30. Ibid. pp. 7-23.
31. *Vanita Vishram Suvarna Mahotsav*, 1915-1965 Poona, 1966, pp.51-60.
32. Khera Vartman, *Native News Paper Report, 1890,* Jan.-Dec. p. 11.
33. *Vanita Vishram Suvarna Mahotsav*, 1915-1965, *Smruti Granth*, Tara Vakil, 'Gujarat nu Gaurav', Poona, 1966, P. 27.
34. Sorabjee Mancherjee Bhagolia (ed); *Stri Gyan Deepak*, Bombay, Union Press, 1868, pp. 1-10.

8

Gender Perceptions in the *Sundri Subodh*, the Popular Women's Journal in Gujarati (1903-1923)

Kunjlata N. Shah

The *Sundari Subodh,* a popular Gujarati monthly journal, was entirely devoted to women. The Bandhu Samaj, a reformist association of Ahmedabad, established it in 1903 in order to uplift women through the print media. The *Sundari Subodh*'s main purpose was to entertain as well as educate the literate middle class women of Gujarat. The Journal aimed at their social, religious, moral and intellectual uplift. It invited women writers to contribute articles, poems and short stories and thus encouraged women's writings.

The members of the Bandhu Samaj were influenced by the traditional patriarchal ideology of the cultural revivalists of Gujarat such as Manibhai Dwivedi, Govardhanram Tripathi and others. They constructed the image of the ideal modern woman rooted in Indian culture and traditions. The magazine became very popular in Gujarat during twenty years of its existence and had a tremendous impact on the sensibilities of Gujarati literate women. The Journal influenced their gender perceptions and also ideas about their own selves.

This paper examines the tone and content of the journal in historical perspective and analyzes women's voices represented in their writings in the *Sundari Subodh* to find out their gender perceptions. The paper probes whether or not the hegemonic patriarchal ideology of the cultural revivalists shaped women's perceptions about themselves and their classes and how far these patriarchal ideas influenced them to formulate their own identities.

I

Social reformers as well as classical revivalists of Gujarat meaningfully used the print media to diffuse their ideas and also to educate and cultivate the minds of literate women of the urban middle class from the 1850s.

The *Sundari Subodh* was not the first women's journal in Gujarati. The *Stree Bodh* or women's wisdom was published as early as 1857 by a group of enlightened Hindu and Parsi social reformers in Mumbai in order to recast the urban middle class women in the Victorian mould of feminine domesticity. Its objective was to provide good quality entertainment and useful education to women. Though started by the social reformers, the contemporary issues of social reform related to women were glaringly absent in it. From the 1880's women contributed stories, poems, and other articles to the Journal. However these women writers adopted and absorbed the concept of Victorian womanhood and accepted their prescribed gender roles as a mother, wife and homemaker.

The second women's magazine in Gujarati, published from Mumbai was the *Stree Mitra*. Parsi women started this illustrated monthly in March 1889. A typical issue featured one or two serialized stories, biographies of European women, and articles on embroidery, stitching, cooking, childcare, health etc. The domestic role of women was emphasized. The *Stree Mitra* was short-lived and ended in1895. The women's writings in both these popular magazines - *Stree Bodh* and *Stree Mitra* - before the First World War did not show any feminist consciousness. Putlibai Kabraji, the editor of the *Stree Bodh* in her article in 1911 wrote that women of India should not imitate western women in demanding rights to vote etc. for that would harm the harmony of family life. Again in 1913 she wrote that women should not compete with men in work and take up only such jobs which were extensions of domestic work.

Here it should be mentioned that an attempt was made by one Tulsibai of the Kheda village to establish *Streesudbodhratna,* a journal for women. However nothing much is known about this magazine.[1]

II

The *Stree Bodh* and *Stree Mitra* were written in Parsi Gujarati and also mainly catered to the needs of urban Parsi middle class women. Hindu and Muslim women read these journals, because there were no other women's journals at that time in Gujarati. Some Gujarati writers and social reformers such as Mahipatram Rupram, Lalshankar Umashankar, H. Kantawala, Krishnarao Bholanath initiated a movement to start a women's magazine in the late 1880's. In 1888, they advertised in the *Gujarat Mitra*, the popular Gujarati newspaper published from Surat, "Though the *Stree Bodh* is a prestigious monthly magazine, it discusses mainly the topics related to the Parsee community. As there is no journal for the Hindu women written by Hindu women, we are planning to start one". However, their efforts were only realized in 1903 when the Bandhu Samaj of Ahmedabad established the *Sundari Subodh.*

The Bandhu Samaj was set up by a group of young educated Nagar Brahmin men such as Bhongindrarao Divetia, Rammohan Rai Desai, Shankarrai Amritrai and others in Ahmedabad in the last decade of the nineteenth century in order to uplift women of Gujarat by developing suitable literature for women in Gujarati. In order to fulfill this purpose, they started to publish the *Sundari Subodh*, a monthly journal, from September 1903.

Ahmedabad at the turn of the twentieth century had emerged not only as a centre of modern textile industry but also as an important centre of education and the socio- religious reform movement in Gujarat. The Gujarat Vernacular Society, established by Alexander Forbes and his British friends in 1848, was the nucleus of the educational, literary and social reform activities of the city. It published the *Buddhi Prakash*, a periodical that propagated new and progressive ideas throughout Gujarat. The Society from the beginning took up the cause of women. It advocated women's education and established the first school for girls in 1850 with generous donations from *shethani* Harkunvar, a rich and enlightened widow of Hatesingh. The axiom of the *Buddhi Prakash* was "No social reform is possible without women's education". Ahmedabad remained in the forefront of women's education in Gujarat in the nineteenth century. The first two women graduates - Vidyaben Nilkanth and her sister Shardaben Mehta- who passed the B. A. examination in 1901 were from Ahmedabad.

Social reformers of Ahmedabad as well as of Gujarat like elsewhere in the country were preoccupied with the "Women's Question" from the mid-nineteenth century. Durgram Mehtaji, Dalpatram, Narmadashankar, Mahipatram Rupram, Bholanath Sarabhai were some of the early reformers of Gujarat who were impressed by western thought and combated evils that debased women. They focussed on the issues such as maltreatment of widows, child-marriage, polygamy, the ban on widow remarriage, dowry, marriage expenses, and obscene wedding songs. These reformists as well as cultural revivalists later had a strong conviction that education of women would reform women and that in turn would reform society and the country. This conviction led to the growth of women's literacy and education in Gujarat.

The emergence of the new middle class was a significant socio-cultural phenomenon in the wake of the economic and social changes brought about by British rule. New administrative, educational and judicial systems, modern financial and commercial institutions and industrialization in the nineteenth century created new occupations that separated home and workplace. The British colonial policy and industrialization shattered the traditional handicraft industries in which women were extensively engaged. As a result, the economic participation of women was reduced and their productive role was adversely affected in the economy. The separation of the workplace and home also created a dichotomy of the public and the private sphere in colonial India. As a result it became necessary for the reformers and revivalists and later nationalists to redefine or re-articulate middle-class Indian womanhood. They reorganized gender roles and division of labour outside and within the family of the middle classes in view of the changing times. The home or *Griha* became the private space, the domain of women as opposed to the outside world, the public space, the sphere of men. Middle class woman in this new scheme was essentially conceived of as a homemaker or *Grihini* who had no economic function to perform or any role to play in the process of production. Her reproductive role in the family was emphasized and her role of mother was glorified.

It is interesting to examine the perceptions of some social reformers and revivalists of Gujarat about womanhood in the nineteenth century. Mahipatram Rupram, (1829-1891) a 'western-oriented' social reformer of Gujarat wrote *Parvatikunvar Akhyan*, the biography of his wife Parvatikunvar, in 1881, immediately after her death. This work gives us an insight into the gender perceptions of Mahipatram, a great supporter of women's cause and their education. Parvatikunvar was a devoted wife who supported Mahipatram in all his reformist activities and stood by him when he was ostracized by his caste when he returned from abroad. Influenced by her husband's reformist and progressive ideas, she herself contributed to the reform movement of Gujarat by encouraging women's education and protesting boldly against the unjust restrictions heaped on the women of Gujarat. He also encouraged her to socialize with the European wives of the British officials. Mahipatram in the biography extols her boldness, courage, and her progressive outlook. However, Mahipatram like other men of his period believed in separate spheres in life for men and women. Influenced by colonial Victorian ideas of femininity and domesticity he perceives Parvatikunvar in the biography, essentially as a domestic angel who is an efficient home-maker and loving wife, who is proficient in cooking, stitching and other household work and takes up all the responsibilities of the household to make her husband free to perform public and professional duties outside home. By using traditional symbolism and calling his devoted wife 'sati' and 'pativrata' Mahipatram reinforces the patriarchal concept of ideal Indian womanhood. He conceives an image of' 'the new woman' in Parvatikunvar who amicably combines traditional and modern features of womanhood. At the end of the biography, he states that the purpose of writing the life of his wife is to present this image of the 'new woman' of Parvatikunvar as a role model for other young women.[2]

The works of Govardhanram Tripathi (1855-1907) a leading cultural revivalist and litterateur of Gujarat had a great impact on the middle class in the nineteenth and the early years of the twentieth century. Govardhanram was a reformer among revivalists who believed in bringing about gradual and moderate changes in society. His epic novel, *Saraswatichandra* in four volumes (1887-1900) is a landmark in Gujarati literature not only for its intrinsic literary value but also for its social influence on Gujarat especially on its middle class. Govardhanram though impressed by western progress and its dynamism, highly respected Indian culture and its traditional values. He created women characters such as Gunsundari, Kumud, and Kusum, who blended in them, the traditional and modern ideals of womanhood. Gunsundari, cast in the Indian traditional mould, especially became a role model for the middle class women of Gujarat. He depicted Gunsundari as an intelligent, warm and virtuous woman, loving wife, caring and understanding mother and a nurturer of a large family, which she managed with great efficiency and frugality. *Sarswatichandra* played a great role in shaping the identity of middle class women at the turn of the twentieth century.

This was the social and ideological climate in Gujarat when the Bandhu Samaj of Ahmedabad started the *Sundari Subodh* in 1903.

III

In the preface of the first issue, September 1903, of the *Sundari Subodh* Rajmohan Desai, the editor, on behalf of the Bandhu Samaj states its origin and objectives.[3] The main purpose of this magazine, he writes, is to fill up the existing lacuna, of not having any journal for Hindu women written in pure Gujarati. The editor further says that though there were journals for women published from Mumbai by Parsi women, they deal with their lifestyles and their way of thinking and were written in Parsi Gujarati. The editor added that the purpose of the Journal was to broaden the vision of women by providing them with knowledge and the news of the country and the world and it also intended to discuss women's education, home decoration, childcare, home medicine, nutrition, health, household tips, domestic crafts such as knitting, embroidery, cooking, issues related to women, biographies of great women, etc. The editor wrote that it would also feature excerpts from foreign and Indian periodicals. The editor emphasized that the language of the periodical would be pure Gujarati but simple so even those less educated women would understand it. He appealed to the men of Gujarat to support the noble cause of the magazine by subscribing to it and making this endeavour a success. The *Sundari Subodh* according to this preface aimed at educating and entertaining the literate middle class women of Gujarat and it wanted to provide them with educative reading material to keep them pleasantly engaged in their leisure time.

In the very first issue, the tone of the journal was set in the article entitled "Grihini Mahima" or the importance of a homemaker in which the author exhorted women to be like Kumud, the heroine of *Saraswatichandra,* who won the love of her in-laws by her warmth and who also tried to reform her debauched husband. He further advised them to be like Gunsundari, another character of the same work, who would welcome her husband returning tired after a hard days work with a smile and entertain him with her wit and pleasant talk.[4]

From the beginning the articles by women writers, just to name a few - Bai Narmadakunvar, Sulochana, Bahen Nisha, Tribhovantanya, Satvamati, Kantida, Chanchallakshmi Joshi - emphatically stated that the duties of the wife were to regard her husband as an *Ishwar* or God. She should try to keep him always happy and should not oppose him as it was against her *Streedharma.* They lauded the concept of a *Pativrata* woman or a devoted wife. Satvamati in the issue of March 1906 wrote that by observing *Pativrata dharma* woman could get liberation or Moksha. One can perceive that these women writers were completely co-opted into the hegemonic fold of patriarchy upheld by the cultural revivalists. These writings show the thoughts prevailing among middle class women in those times and reveal that they had internalized the patriarchal ideology and accepted their subservient position in the family. Many men writers in the Journal also reiterated these ideas and reinforced the patriarchal ideology.

Most of the articles written by women and men accepted and absorbed the doctrine of two spheres - public and private. Mangla Gauri Chunilal Setalwad in the article entitled *Stree purushna karyo* or duties of men and women, in the issue of December 1909, said that men and women had separate areas of work. Even if a woman was educated and intelligent she should not neglect her duties as a housewife and a mother and she should not compete with men. Karanlal Dhruv wrote in the issue of November 1909, that in outside work, a woman could not work independently without the help of a man. A woman could not become a *neta* or leader but could only become a *mantri* or a secretary. However, he further said that in the housework and family matters woman was the master. Thus the home or *Griha* was perceived as the private sphere, the domain of a *Grihini* or homemaker. Home was the kingdom where the husband was a king and she was a minister. In some articles a higher status of Queen was endowed on her.[5] Chanchallakshmi, in the issue of April 1913, enumerated the virtues of a housewife, which included *Pativrata*, seriousness, hard work, cleanliness, good nature, good company, practical wisdom, and frugality.

The periodical was reformist but conservative in its outlook. It protested against child marriage and unnecessary customs, superstitions etc. It championed the cause of women's education and also supported inter-caste marriages. When Babu Bhupendranath Basu's Bill of Civil Marriage was heatedly debated, the *Sundari Subodh* expressed the opinion favouring it. However, it did not favour widows or even widower's remarriage. It upheld the ideal of monogamy and *Pativrata*. Kantida, a woman writer said in her article in the issue of October 1909, that widow remarriage was against the ideal of *Pativrata* and thus it was immoral. The *Sundari Subodh* published the speech of Naniben Gajjar, the founder of the Vanita Samaj in the issue of April 1908 in which she said that widows should not marry but should study and be self-sufficient.

The Journal glorified woman's role as a mother in home and family. In each issue, articles on childcare, housekeeping, health, and home-medicine were featured. The *Sundari Subodh* conceived an ideal woman as a mother and housewife, devoted to home, family, and husband. It did not visualize woman as an individual having her own separate identity. A good homemaker and gentle wife was preferred to a good orator and scholar[6].

The *Sundari Subodh* emphasized that woman should be educated so that she would perform her role as a wife, mother and homemaker in more efficient way. An educated mother according to many articles written by women and men could take care of her children in a responsible manner and also could give them education of morals etc. at home and thus through their children especially sons she could improve the future of the nation. The periodical frequently carried articles by women and men explaining the adverse effects of uneducated mothers on the family and children. Jiviben Nanji wrote a series of articles entitled "The effects of uneducated mothers on children" in 1904. She appealed to all Indians to educate women in order to uplift the nation. Nisha from Gondal also echoed these views in her articles.

A debate over the curriculum for girls arose in the last decade of the nineteenth century in Gujarat. Many educationists like Lalshankar Umashankar, Nilkanthrai Chhatrapati, and Kamlashankar Pranshankar Trivedi believed that women's education should be useful to women to make them better homemakers and mothers. Thus these educationists wanted to include subjects like home-management, childcare, hygiene, healthcare etc. in the curriculum for girls. Mr. Chimanlal Setalwad, a leading lawyer, was of the opinion that female education should be utilitarian and should suit woman's nature. He further argued that to train them as lawyers and to place them in competition with men would not benefit either.[7]

This debate on the content of the girls' education was carried on very enthusiastically in the articles written both by men and women in the *Sundari Subodh* from the beginning. In these heated discussions about the nature and scope of the curriculum suitable for women, we can clearly see the gender perceptions of men as well as women writers. Behn Nisha from Gondal in the issues of July and August 1905 writes that the curriculum for women should include *Vaidak Shastra* or indigenous medicine, the knowledge of foreign and Indian languages, *Dharmaniti* or a code of conduct, cooking, duties towards husband and in-laws etc. Sulochana, another woman writer also in the issue of July 1905, agreed with Nisha on most of the points but added accounts and childcare in the curriculum. Krshnagauri Hiralal Rawal in the issue of December 1907 wrote that women should be given education that would be useful in her life and home. She emphatically said that *Kanyashala*s should teach cooking and nutrition to girls. Bhogindrarao Divetia, an active member of the Bandhu Samaj wrote in the *Sundari Subodh* that education should make a woman good wife and mother and a girl in the school should be taught stitching, knitting, healthcare, elementary chemistry, cooking, the scriptures, biographies of great men and women and she should also be taught her duties towards her husband, parents, and in-laws.[8] The majority of men and women writers in the Journal conceived women's education and upliftment within the confines of the domestic sphere. However, Vidhyaben Nilkanth and her sister Shardaben Mehta had a different viewpoint. They were of the opinion that women's education should not be different from men's. Vidhyaben writes that though in life men and women have different fields of interest, they should be given similar kind of education because women and men have equal intellectual capacities. Shardaben also wrote that a woman should be taught History, Geography and other subjects to develop her intellect and education should be in harmony with our culture.[9]

The *Sundari Subodh* became the most readable family magazine in the first two decades of the twentieth century. From 1912 the journal was illustrated with photographs and pictures. From 1917 Gandhiji's activities, national songs featured regularly. Krishnagauri Rawal wrote in the issue of December 1912 that the *Sundari Subodh* was so useful and interesting to women that every family should subscribe to it. The *Sundari Subodh* created a wide sphere of social influence in the middle class of Gujarat in first quarter of the twentieth century.

References

1. Kunjlata Shah, "Women's Journals in Gujarati (1857-1947)", S.Shirgaonkar. C. Parsure, M. Kamerkar, U. Apte (eds.), in *Streejeevan Vishayak Sthityantar: Mumbai Parisar (1876 - 1950),* Mumbai, 1992, pp. 215-222. Sonal Shukla, "Cultivating Minds: 19th Century Gujarati women's Journals, *Economic and Political Weekly,* October 26, 1991, pp. WS-63-66.
2. Mahpatram Rupram, *Parvatikunvar Akhyan* (in Gujarati), Ahmedabad, 1881, passim.
3. *Sundari Subodh*, September 1903, pp. 4-7.
4. *Ibid.* pp. 10-12.
5. *Ibid.*
6. *Ibid.* December 1904, p. 76.
7. *Gujarat Shalapatra*, January 1897, pp.30-36, February 1897, p. 41.
8. *Sundari Subodh*, April 1907, pp.182-186.
9. *Ibid.* January 1912, pp. 169-173

9

Institution Building and Social Change in Western India: A Case Study of Vanita Vishram, Surat, 1907-1920

Makrand Mehta

Introduction

Institutions are shaped by the perceptions and the objectives of the actors in a given historical situation. While breathing the existing socio-cultural and economic environment, they pave the way for a change. The objective of this paper is to analyse the activities of the Vanita Vishram founded by two child widows in Surat in 1907 for the uplift of the widows and the destitutes. This was before Gandhi emerged as a national leader.

The British rule generated progressive ideas and also created educated middle class. For this reason, the nineteenth and the early twentieth century witnessed social reform movements, often focussing on women's issues. A large number of women like Harkunvar, Pandita Ramabai, Ramabai Ranade, Anandibai Joshi, Krishna Gauri Rawal, Tarabai Shinde, Motiben Kapadia, and Mary and Cornelia Sorabji stepped forward and fought against patriarchy and gender discrimination.[1] There is a corpus of theoretical and empirical literature shedding light on the gender approaches. It seems, however, that there are few systematic accounts of women's grass-roots organization before the Gandhian period, focussing on the nature of organizational leadership, the style of communication and the nature and direction of change. Many such organizations such as the Arya Mahila Sabha, Gujarat Ladies' Club, Seva Sadan and the Gujarati Hindu Stree Mandal existed in Western India in the pre-Gandhian period. The Vanita Vishram was one of them. I argue that the perceptions and methods of its organizers differed from those of the Western-educated intelligentsia who were then advocating rights and social justice for women.

Antecedents of the Vanita Vishram

The British established not only political but also cultural hegemony. The first generation of well-to-do women, cherishing Western liberal and rational ideas were dazzled to see in their home towns how their British counterparts were walking side-by-side with males, and mixing freely with them in the public. No distinctive marks for the widows! On the contrary British women including widows were known to be enjoying equal rights with men. This was really awe-inspiring. Naturally therefore, Indian women launched a crusade against child marriage, disfiguring of the widows, restrictions on the marriage of child widows, dowry system and breast-beatings on the occasion of death. In Ahmedabad, women formed their own institution, the Gujarat Ladies' Club, in 1888.[2] The members included Mary and Cornelia Sorabji, Vidyagauri Nilkanth, Dr. Motiben Kapadia, Gnyanandadevi Satyendranath Tagore and Mrs. Gopal Hari Deshmukh. The members also included the wives of local British bureaucrats and teachers of the Female Training College. These ladies read newspapers and journals, played tennis and also organized picnics and seminars.[3] This phenomenon was unprecedented. The coming together of well-meaning and well-informed women cutting across caste and community lines was something new. The speeches and the writings and the campaigns of these women softened the cage of the age-old customs and conventions.

But with all said and done, the activities of the intellectuals did not help the widows and the other oppressed women beyond a point. It came out as an open secret that a large number of widow marriages had failed, and even led to the further humiliation of the remarried widows. As a contemporary journal observed:

> 'Our well-to-do educated women articulate women's issues in a wonderful way. But they have little practical experience. They should do something more concrete for the actual development of women.'[4]

These observations were not totally unjustified. Even Vidyagauri Nilkanth, a noted social reformer and the first woman Graduate of Gujarat (1901) was unaware of the grass root activities of the Ahmedabad and the Surat Vanita Vishram. She came to know only after she received an invitation from the Ahmedabad Vanita Vishram (founded in 1907 itself on the Surat model) to preside over its gathering in March 1910.[5] In her speech Vidyaben confessed that there was little rapport between women like her and grass roots workers and that there should be meaningful dialogues between all sorts of women engaged in the developmental activities. It seems that the Vanita Vishram was the culmination of the earlier movements and a more mature and complex phase at that period of time.

Genesis of the Vanita Vishram

The founders of the Vanita Vishram, Bajigauri Munshi (1867-1926) and Shivgauri (alias Naniben) Gajjar (1871-1945) were child widows. Bajigauri belonged to the prestigious Nagar caste known for its literary and administrative tradition. Her parents, Mahimangauri and Daulatram Munshi were well read and held progressive views. Naniben belonged to the Vaisha Suthar caste. Her father, Kalyandas, was a rich timber merchant, and brother, Tribhuvandas, a well-known scientist. The family members of these widows decided to send them to a school and they soon became friends.

Tribhuvandas Gajjar (1863-1920) had studied in Bombay's Elphinstone College. He then joined the Baroda College as a professor of Chemistry in 1888. Two years later he established Kala Bhavan, which has now grown into the Faculty of Technology of the Maharaja Sayajirao University of Baroda. He had invented some drugs and medicines during the disastrous famine of 1899-1900 and had distributed them free to the people affected by the plague.[6] He maintained a diary. The following entry dated 14 July 1888 provides useful insights into the antecedents of the Vanita Vishram. The diary states:

> "Science and technology are parts of the same coin. But what the Country needs today is applied science. This will help the poor country from further exploitation. I want to use my technological know-how for the services of the people. 'Live for others' is the motto of my life. Nani is now 17 and it is difficult for me to bear her pains. I must do something so that she can live a dignified life".[7]

The Vanita Vishram was the result of long and careful deliberations between Bajigauri, Naniben and their family members. The project involved a lot of money and moral responsibility, besides skills. The founders were all familiar with the activities of D. K. Karve, B. M. Malbari, Pandita Ramabai, Ramabai Ranade, Kashibai Devdhar and Jamnaben Sakkai. They knew about the activities of the Arya Mahila Sabha (Poona, 1893), Anath Balika Ashram (Poona, 1897), Gujarati Hindu Stree Mandal (Bombay, 1903) and Seva Sadan (Bombay, 1906). Their role models were, however, Karve, Ramabai Ranade and Jamnaben, not the fiery Malbari and Pandita Ramabai. Naniben and Bajigauri had earlier come into contact with Jamnaben Sakkai, the founder of the Gujarati Hindu Stree Mandal.[8] They had developed good rapport with this old and experienced woman.

This institution was thus the result of the teamwork among the family members of the widows and other knowledgeable people having love, faith and respect for each other. The initial funds were as follows:

Naniben Gajjar's parents donated a house and 6,000 rupees; Professor Gajjar Rs. 4,000; Bajigauri's parents Rs.

6,000. In keeping with the Gujarati Hindu tradition, Bajigauri and Naniben had acquired the pallu amount. They parted with the entire amount, Bajigauri's 3000 rupees and Naniben's 6000 rupees.[9] This made a total of 25,000 rupees plus a suitable house to run the institution. The Vanita Vishram, was the result of the untiring zeal, enthusiasm and sacrifice of these widows. It was inaugurated on May 15, 1907 with great enthusiasm and hopes.

Growth and Expansion

The Vanita Vishram started with two widows and seven girls. The self-denying and self-effacing image of the organizers had enabled them to win the hearts of the students' parents. Fortunately many students and inmates have left accounts showing how they developed themselves as self-employed entrepreneurs after they left their 'real home'. One of the widows, Parvatiben Desai (1897 – 1975) states:

'I joined the Vanita Vishram in the very first year. The whole city knew that Bajigauriben and Naniben were real **sadhvis** who had given up personal desires. My parents, therefore, did not hesitate to entrust me to their care. When we went to this **ashram,** we found two women in simple white dress with shaven heads. They welcomed me with profound affection and asked me some questions. My parents then returned home and I started weeping. Today I am the Superintendent of the same institution which I had seen some fifty years ago. I had learnt my first lessons of love, compassion and self-reliance in this **ashram.**[10]

Education was free in the Vanita Vishram, and there were nominal charges for the inmates. This together with the institution's teaching and training programmes attracted girls and elderly women to the Vanita Vishram. Professor T. K. Gajjar who had earlier established the Kala Bhavan in Baroda helped the Vanita Vishram in designing some vocational courses such as sewing, tailoring, embroidery work, mechanical drawing and carpentry. He also donated a few machines and equipment for this purpose. The students learnt how to make folders, cardboards and envelopes of different shapes and sizes.

The Vanita Vishram also taught languages, science, arithmetic and other subjects of academic value.

As the students turned out by the Vanita Vishram started earning as self-employed artisan–entrepreneurs, the institution became very popular. In 1914 the management had to shift to a bigger house in order to accommodate the swelling number of students. Funds started pouring in from the Surat and the Bombay entrepreneurs such as Naginchand Jhaveri, Sir Purshottamdas Thakurdas, and Sir Vitthaldas Damodardas Thackersey. Naniben had earlier come into contact with Nathibai Damodardas Thackersey through her brother and Jamnaben Sakkai. The house constructed in 1914 has now turned into a big educational and training complex with vast land.

The Vanita Vishram was also innovative in some other respects. It started a journal, the **Vanita Vignyan** in 1909 with a view to providing useful information on arts, crafts, science and technology. The articles written in simple Gujarati provided useful information along with the visuals. In terms of management, the work was informally divided, Bajigauri looking after the routine work and Naniben touring in Gujarat to propagate the institution's mission. The Annual Reports of the Vanita Vishram and also the contemporary files of **Gujarat Mitra** (Surat) and **Prajabandhu** give ample proof of Naniben's ability to carry home her views. The report of **Prajabandhu** dated January 17, 1909 shows how she addressed the women's gathering in Nadiad, Ahmedabad, Baroda, Rajkot, Bhavnagar and as far as the remote towns of Bhuj and Anjar in Kachchh. Naniben continued her visits to Gujarat. The Vanita Vishrams of Nadiad (1916), Rajkot (1921), Siddhpur and Bhavnagar (1924) and Porbandar (1928) were mainly due to her missionary work. It is worth noting that unlike the Western-educated women, she used religious idioms and phrases to convince her listeners that her main intention in using the collective force was to raise the quality of life and working condition of the oppressed women. Actually she was fighting for equality and justice.

The numerous articles published by Naniben and Bajigauri in newspapers like **Gujarat Mitra** and journals like **Sundari Subodh** show how forthright they were in influencing the readers.

Conclusion

This survey shows that by the beginning of the twentieth century women's agitations had created great awareness in the society with regard to the issues that adversely affected women. But transforming reform into more viable concrete action required different vision and skills. The Vanita Vishram filled up this gap and in this respect it was the forerunner of the later movements for change at the institutional level. Its stance was 'social work' rather than 'reform'. For this reason, perhaps, it won the mass support and built up the careers of many oppressed and needy women.

References

1. For details see Susie Tharu and K. Lalitha (eds.) *Women Writing in India: 600 B.C. to the Present* Delhi, 1995; Uma Chakravarti, *Rewriting History: The Life and Times of Pandita Ramabai*, New Delhi, 1998
2. Makrand Mehta, 'Gujaratnin Pratham, Mahila Sanstha: The Gujarat Ladies' Club', *Samipya* April 1994 – September 1994, Pp. 63-69.
3. Makrand Mehta and Shirin Mehta, "Bhomia Vina Sangharsha Yatra, Oganisama Saikanin Tran Vidhvaonun Parshvadarsham" *Paryaya*, January – June, 1995, pp. 1-15; Shirin Mehta, 'Gujarati Society and Women', Key-note Address, *Gujarat Itihas Parishad*, Mumbai, December, 1995.
4. *Sundari Subodh*, Vol. 4, no. 2, October 1906, P. 59.
5. Vidyagauri's speech on the occasion of the monthly gathering of the Vanita Vishram held on 10th June 1910. Source: *Annual Report of the Ahmedabad Vanita Vishram* for the year 1909-1910.
6. Makrand Mehta, 'Science Verses Technology: The Early years of Kala Bhavan, Baroda, 1890-1896,' *Indian Journal of History of Science*, Vol. 27, No. 2, 1992, PP. 146-169.
7. *Gajjar Records*.
8. Speeches of Bajigauri Munshi and Naniben (Shivgauri) Gajjar at the time of the inauguration ceremony of the Surat Vanita Vishram on May 15, 1907. Source: *Gujarat Mitra* (Surat) dated May 17, 1907.

9. Naniben Gajjar, 'Gujaratnan Stree Mandalo: Vanita Vishramnan Anubhavo', *Vasant*, No. 10, Samvat 1967-68 (A. D. 1910-11), pp. 204-07.
10. Pamphlet titled 'Vanita Vishramnin Adya Sansthapako' published by the Vanita Vishram in November 1959.

10

Lokahitwadi—Harbinger of Social Change

Usha Thakkar

Gopal Hari Deshmukh (1823-1892) known as Lokahitwadi (the proponent of what is good for the people) belonged to the generation in the nineteenth century India which was the first to admire the wonders of the West, and to criticize the traditional setup of the Indian Society. He admired the British rule and was happy with the advantages received by the Indians under it, such as the increasing technological advances and the initiation of progressive social ideas and legislations. The times he witnessed were tumultuous and the society he lived in was in the grip of oppressive traditions. Still his ideas transcended the narrow limits of traditions and customs, and he presented a vision for a new society rooted in rationalism and human values.

Some members of the newly educated class like him discovered to their considerable distress that the society which had bred them, and about which they often boasted, was not an ideal one, but ridden with many evils, untouchability, poverty, inequality, discrimination against and ill treatment of women. Eventually, it dawned upon them that a fresh look at the past was essential. They started having doubts about the validity of the accepted norms of social conduct in India, which they felt were not supported by reason and the universal values of humanity. The arrival of the British created a major upheaval. For the first time, Indian society as a whole felt an external impact in all its facets, and the new elite that came to take up the cudgels for change were faced with the arduous task of harmonizing seemingly contradictory and disparate cultural impulses.

The challenge facing the educated elite of the country in the second half of the nineteenth century was unprecedented. On one hand there was the Indian society - hierarchical, rooted in caste-discriminations and untouchability, and permitting the oppression of women by customs like sati and forced widowhood. On the other hand there was the West - with its dazzling ideas of equality and freedom, aiming at the greatest happiness of the greatest number, and demanding human treatment for all. The temptation was to claim that one could harmonize the traditional and the progressive. Probing minds like that of Lokahitwadi gave voice to the restlessness that had started troubling them.

Lokahitwadi, born in 1823, came from a Pune Brahman Sardar family with the surname Shidhaye. His father was one among the troops that accompanied Bajirao II in his flight from Pune in 1818. His father's death in 1836 made young Gopal aware of the harshness of life. Gopal studied at the Pune Government English School from 1841-1844, and earned praise from his teachers. He joined the government service, and worked in the judicial and revenue departments. He was posted in various places of Bombay Presidency like Pune, Wai, Bombay, Nashik and Ahmedabad. He worked from 1855 to 1861 for the Inam Commission, which dealt with the claims of the holders of the Inam and the hereditary landlords. Thereafter for a year he was appointed by the government to prepare a digest of laws from the Hindu and Mohammedan religions books in Bombay. He was appointed by the Government in 1862 as Assistant Judge for Ahmedabad, but the protest from the British officials proved to be an obstacle. Then he served as Small Causes Judge at Nashik and later at Ahmedabad where he stayed for almost eleven years. He retired in 1878 as Sessions Judge. He received distinctions and honours towards the end of his government service. He was appointed Justice of Peace, Rao Bahadur and Fellow of the University of Bombay. In 1880 he became a member of the Legislative Council of Bombay and in the following year, a First Class Sardar. After retirement in 1880 he spent most of the remaining twelve years of his life in Pune.

Lokahitwadi left an indelible print on the social history of Maharashtra in the later half of the nineteenth century because of his well-argued and logical writings as well as his commitment to social reform. His long association with M. G. Ranade was mutually enriching and nurturing. When he left Ahmedabad, Mohanlal Dalapatram, a poet, wrote a long poem in Gujarati in his praise. His multi faceted personality puts him apart from other reformers and thinkers of the period. As pointed out by M.R. Lederle, "It is not possible to sum up the activities and ideas of Lokahitwadi under any one ism."[1] He knew the complexities of old Peshwa rule and had experienced the tensions of the new British rule. His knowledge extended from Hindu religions, textbooks and Mohammedan and Parsi sacred books to the important intellectual works in English. He was a member of the Prarthana Samaj, for a few years even its president. He knew Dayanand Saraswati and was involved with the activities of the Arya Samaj. He also was in touch with the Theosophical circles. He continued the liberal tradition of Elphinstone and B. G. Jambhekar, exhorting the people to become national and to accept modern learning.[2] He prepared the ground for the awakening in Maharashtra around 1870s and was a leader of ideological revolution.[3]

He remained active and engaged throughout his life, in the activating of reading, writing, propagating new ideas, encouraging establishment of schools and libraries, taking up causes of social reform, giving help and medicine to the sick and the needy, advocating the idea of 'Swadeshi' (made in our own country) goods, and even visualizing Parliament in India, consisting only of the wisest, irrespective of religion, caste or foreign/indigenous origin. He wrote 39 books and many articles in newspapers and journals.[4] The topics ranged from History, ancient texts, religion, to social reform, education, economic issues and social condition. In Arun Joshi's words, he was "living history of Maharashtra of those times."[5]

An attempt is made in this paper to focus on his views on the condition of women and to highlight how he brought women's issues to the agenda of social reform. The first section provides the main tenets of his approach, the second discusses his views on marriage and the third presents his views on widow-remarriage and the fourth on women's education. The last section contains concluding comments.

Approach

Lokahitwadi's importance lay in the fact that he did not follow the much-traversed path of traditions and preferred to carve his niche by his appeal to reason. In a society like that of India religion has played a dominant role in the life of the people. It is a central concept tying together the beads of individual happiness and social togetherness. In addition the hold of the past is very strong. Almost any attempt to interpret or understand the present has to be done in the context of her past. It is this context which made, and continues to make, Lokahitwadi special. He was quick to perceive the hollowness of many Indian traditions and rituals. With rare boldness, he expressed the view that it was high time that we all decided our way. Rituals were of no use, but morality (Niti) was the right path to follow. What was needed was purity of heart, will to change and determination to follow strategies, which could change the outlook of the people.[6]

In his introduction to "Nigam Prakash" he wrote, "It is necessary that Reformers, in order to be successful, ought to possess knowledge of the ancient literature, which the people have, through habit, ignorance and Priest-craft learned to venerate...The Religion of a nation greatly affects its destinies and progress. Adherence to the ancient prejudices combined with the thickly prevailing ignorance and a powerful priest-craft has produced baneful effects, such as early marriages, miserable and forced widowhood, prevention of traveling to foreign countries, slavery of female sex, waste of money on useless objects, eleemosynary habits of one-tenth of the population, internal dissentions, want of fellow-feeling and patriotism and above all false worship of God. When reformers try to remove these effects, where do they stumble? At the religious difficulty."[7]

Lokahitwadi's hundred and eight bold articles on religious, educational, economic, social and women's issues published in "Prabhakar" (from Mumbai) during March 1848 to May 1850, were trendsetters. He urged his readers to discard hackneyed traditions supported by the selfish Brahmins and exhorted them to think independently so that they would understand the gravity of social evils and the pathetic condition of women. His arguments were intended to evoke the reasoning ability in the individual. He believed that, "Let it be the saying of Manu or Yajnavalkya or even Brahmadeva, It is the reasoning which is powerful. Keep the Shastras aside, use your mind, think and then proceed".[8] He propagated the dictum "Buddhireva Baliyasi" (Reasoning is powerful). His appeal to his readers was sincere and passionate.

His fervent appeal to his readers was, "I request all you people to begin to think, to develop habit of reading, to read new books and newspapers and observe what is happening around you. Begin to realize that the British have many good qualities. ...Compared with your ancient sciences, books, opinions and ideas a hundred times better and as many more sciences have now arisen. Examine them all. In your regard for wealth, do not stick to your laziness. Know that the bhatts and pandits are just fools. Search for true morality."[9] Learning meant knowledge, which made a person pure, rational and capable.[10]

M.R. Lederle emphasizes: "The Shatpatre represents an outspoken, impatient, penetrating analysis of the ills of society. *Svadhyaya athava Aryavidyancha Krama, Vichara ani Parikshana*, published in 1880, and more moderate in its diction, gives the opinion of the experienced, mature reformer. The Shatpatre and Svadhyaya hold the key to an understanding of Lokhitwadi." [11]

Lokahitwadi's approach to women's issues is full of compassion and humanity. At the same time, we can see that it is rooted in the concepts of liberation, equality and justice, which were rather unusual for his times. After him, Phule, Vishnushastri Pandit and Agarkar developed similar ideas.

Lokahitwadi's arguments are logical and direct. He maintained that the condition of a nation's people was bound to be bad, if they were not willing to honour the rights of women. In the distant past, women enjoyed a high status in almost all matters. But then with the coming of the Muslims, the ways of the Hindus also changed, and their views regarding women were affected adversely. Hindu society fell prey to foolish and wicked ways and neglected the welfare of its women. Their knowledge was limited to superstitions such as the view that there was no limit to the universe, and that there was a sea of milk. They were perhaps not even aware of international events such as the revolution in France, the evolution of Parliament in England, the fall of the Roman Empire, the migration of Europeans in large number to America. Such people became incapable of reasoning, and were like animals. In these circumstances it was extremely difficult to bring about changes in the position of women. It would take a century or two to create an adequate consciousness of their condition among the people and two or three generations after his own, if the appropriate knowledge was disseminated. He believed that men would have to be wise and then women would also be wise.[12]

Lokahitwadi wrote boldly that the pitiable condition of women, their status like that of animals, their life devoid of knowledge, and cruelty of men had continued existence in our society based on the ancient texts, but now there should be an end to all these, as women were equal to men.[13] He was clear that we must implement the dictum that women have the same rights as those of men, and hence widows were free to remarry.[14]

He visualized a society, where men and women would benefit by each other's company. In his opinion interaction of women with men would have a sobering effect on men's behaviour and speech, because women were pure and inclined to religion and faith. Men were street-smart and knew the ways of the world. Women would receive information through them and good qualities and purity would touch men by keeping women's company.[15] The crime of female infanticide was spine-chilling to all sensitive human beings. Expressing his views against this heinous crime, Lokahitwadi wrote, "Women are weak and entitled to protection from men. Their rights and privilege are coequal with those of men and children are much more so from innocence and helplessness... But what can we say of him who kills his daughter? In what language can we point his wretched heart? He is certainly a monster for he serves to oppose his nature and to stifle the cravings of humanity. Man should exult if he is blessed with a child but on the other hand the inhabitants of Kutch and Kathiawar, the Jariya Rajputs, become sorry when a daughter is born in their house contrary to the custom of sensible men who rejoice equally in the birth of daughter or son."[16] In the times when the lives of women were considered of little consequence, Lokahitwadi had the courage and conviction to state that "In the scale of creation male and female are the same as regards their temporal and spiritual rights. It is only amongst the vulgar and barbarous men that women are considered lower than men but among civilized men great respect is shown to the fair sex...Women possess faculties and capabilities equal to those of men and we have heard several stories of the achievements of women...Women seem to possess greater smoothness of the heart. Their sensibility and tenderness exceeds those of men."[17]

Marriage

Lokahitwadi was aware of the customs governing the institutions of marriage in the Hindu society, which crushed the very existence of women. The Hindus followed the customs of early marriage for their daughters, between the age of eight and ten. Hence the girls did not have any chance to study. Moreover, they believed in horoscopes, and got their daughters married within their own groups in the caste. The study. Moreover, they believed in horoscopes, and got their daughters married within their own groups in the caste. The cumulative result of these factors was that it became difficult to get a proper match, and often a girl's life was wasted. She could become a widow and then have to tolerate insults from the in-laws for life. Lokahitwadi was pained to observe the way the Hindus subjected their women to a life of low status and misery. He was acutely aware of the low status of women and oppressive customs pertaining to their marriage.[18]

He believed that girls should never be forced into marriage. "If according to some, this does not have the support of our religious texts, we shall have to change our texts, and we ourselves shall have to assume the role of Rishis (seers and law-makers). A girl is married young, so she cannot study; and then she lands into trouble. As an old person saying that he cannot take any medicine though needed, because his mother is not there to give it, is liable to be ridiculed, we also today do not talk sense, if we decided to follow hackneyed rules and customs."[19]

Lokahitwadi was aware of the fact that early marriage for both boys and girls brought miseries to them and to the children born to them. In his opinion, "our people are short-lived, devoid of prowess and foolish because of this evil practice."[20] In fact parents should take up the responsibility of only making the children wise. They would marry on their own. Parents should not worry about that. "What is the use of throwing the girl on the boy who is jobless, immature and without any inclination about his future, and thereby ruining young life?"[21]

In an age, when the whole society was in the clutches of the oppressive traditions and ritualistic Brahmins, Lokahitwadi's views brought freshness and new vitality. He was clear that a girl's childhood ought to be spent in gaining education, and later at her reaching twenty years of age or so, once she was old enough to understand, she should be married. "Many old men at present marry young girls; if women are granted freedom to marry on their own, why would they marry such old, useless men?"[22]

Lokahitwadi traced the origin of the custom of child-marriage to laziness and lethargy originating from easy way of life. When life was devoid of any work or challenge, and when there was no urge to see other places and add to knowledge, people tended to get their children married at an early age with a view to check vices in them. But the results were disastrous. Quoting the views of the Sanskrit texts, Lokahitwadi showed that there was hardly any proof of child marriage.[23]

His suggestions to bring changes in the repressive customs pertaining to marriage included: relaxing rules regarding marriages among groups in the same caste, not following the rules of astrology regarding marriages very strictly, not spending lavishly on marriages, and relaxing the custom regarding age-limit of girls for marriage and permitting widow remarriages.[24]

Widow-remarriage

Lokahitwadi was one of the most vocal critics of the orthodox Brahmins. Though a Brahmin by birth, he criticized the hypocrisy and ignorance of Brahmins as a class. He chose them as his target of criticism because he believed that as other castes would always follow the Brahmins (the elite class) it was important to start religious and social reforms by evaluating their ways. This factor led him to pay much attention to social reforms such as widow-remarriage, which were relevant more to Brahmins than to other groups in Hindu society. He also criticized feudal lords and other rich social parasites. He showed how Brahmins used religious doctrines and rituals for their selfish purposes. He brought to light for the first time the part played by Brahmins in increasing the sufferings of widows. He exposed Brahmins as the culprits in the opposition to widow-remarriage. According to him, it was sheer injustice in our society that widows were not permitted to remarry. God created women and men equal, and their rights were equal. Then why did such oppression and subjugation exist that permitted men to remarry but not women?[25]

He understood the mind-set of the people living in the rigid social structure. According to him earlier the Hindus were naïve and listened to the Pandits who told widows to climb on the funeral pyre of their dead husbands (and be Satis). People accepted such advice and burnt alive their own daughters-in-law, daughters, sisters-in-law. Such persons by their oppression of widows proved that they were demons.[26] Lokahitwadi was against the custom of Sati, prevalent among the high castes of the Brahmins, Kshatriyas and Vaishyas. He was anguished to find that the way women in our country were oppressed and tortured had no parallel anywhere in the world. They were insulted, criticized, made to starve, tortured and not allowed to remarry, if widowed. Men, on the other hand, could marry as many times as they wanted and at any age they wanted.[27]

Commenting on the sad plight of the child-widow, Lokahitwadi drew a vivid picture of her pathetic life. Neither the in-laws family nor the natal family wanted her, people insulted her, and deprived of good food and bed, she lived in sheer austerity. "Even an animal in the butcher's home does not suffer such a pitiable fate. The butcher puts knife only once, and the suffering is only at that particular moment."[28] Lokahitwadi was aware that the widows were forced to shave their heads, to look ugly and to live without any provision for food and maintenance. The Shastris and Pandits propagated that the plight of the widows was due to their sins in the previous birth.[29]

Himself a scholar of the ancient Sanskrit texts, Lokahitwadi questioned the invincibility of such texts. His logical argument was that the Shastras were for people's happiness. If there was something in them that was against common humanity, there was no harm in putting it aside. With a view to the welfare of the people, the practice of widow remarriage had to be accepted.[30]

Lokahitwadi threw a rational challenge to the argument put forward by the Pandits that widow-remarriage was not permitted by the Manusmriti. He put forth the argument that if Manu had an element of God in him, then "why did he not create an order by which no Brahmin woman's husband will die and she would die before her husband". If he had established such order on this earth, Manu could be called God and whatever the Brahmins did would have been accepted. But that did not happen.[31]

Lokahitwadi studied the ancient Hindu texts and found arguments in favour of widow-remarriage, and appreciated the efforts of Ishwarchandra Vidyasagar, Vishnubuva Brahmachari, Vishnushastri Pandit and Dayananda Saraswati.[32] He showed that widow-remarriage in fact was not against the dictums of the Shastras.[33]

Exposing the myth of the Hindu superiority, he elaborated that the long Brahman rule did not stop the Sati system or infanticide. In those times some burnt women, some buried them alive, some put stones around their necks and drowned them in water. "Did at any time the Hindus stop all this? Never."[34] He criticized the opinion of the Kalyanonnayak Mandali that the widows must follow the routine of eating only once, not eating delicious food, fasting and visiting places of pilgrimage. If a widow, who had gone for abortion, was brought to a Pandit-judge, she was given punishment as if she were a criminal. He would not, for a moment, think (about the situation that led her to this) that the crime of a woman is to be seen in that social context. "The Hindus have exploited the illiterate and poor women. When these women are educated, they will undoubtedly have their accounts squared with the Pandits."[35]

One had to change with the times, as in the area of medicine. This had to be followed in other fields like astrology and Dharamshastra, i.e. moral science. What deserved to be erased had to be nullified. People would have to discard the Shastras, which were against their happiness. Laws pertaining to marriage were not Dharma but customs. They were framed to bring order among people. Once it was noticed that they are not good, there was no harm in replacing them. "Today we all witness the evils of denying widow remarriage, and we should change the law to suit the need of our times."[36] In fact, the death of a husband was not in the hands of a woman. If it were said to the Brahmins that they would have to die when the sacred thread they wore on their body was broken, how would they react? Similarly, women should not be asked to live a life of misery on loss of their husbands.[37]

Lokahitwadi was far ahead of his times in stressing the rights of women. For him, the main advantage of widow-remarriage was precisely that, for it established the equal rights of men and women. He was clear in emphasizing that women ought to get those rights related to life and happiness, which had so far been with men only. His words demand attention even today: "Decide that women have rights equal to men. Women should study. It is good if men and women marry knowingly, and women whose husbands have died may marry again."[38] His logical argument was, "If I made a rule that a man, whose wife dies, will have to renounce the world, he will have to stay outside his house, and his activities pertaining to his work or business will stop. And if I had the power to implement this rule what would men say?"[39]

Pointing out the adverse effects of opposing widow-remarriage, he drew attention to the fact that many babies were killed because widow-remarriages were not allowed. The number was high, almost a hundred in one district. This was like the situation in Kutch and Kathiawad where infant girls were killed.[40] Widow remarriage would lessen immoral liaisons.[41] Aware of the limitations of the society he lived in, Lokhitwadi in his representation to Governor dated May 26 1848 on "Miseries of Crimes Incidental to Brahmin Widowhood: With Suggestions for Their Removal" portrayed a vivid picture of the helplessness of the Hindu widows. Not content with the criticisms against the evil custom of not allowing widow remarriage, Lokahitwadi gave concrete suggestions to sensitize the society against this evil. These suggestions included steps to encourage essays with rewards on the subject of widow-remarriage in schools and colleges, especially Sanskrit colleges and establishment of Widow's Fund for encouraging men to marry widows.[42]

Lokahitwadi realized that the issue of helplessness of widows was important in Maharashtra in nineteenth century, as the sati issue was in Bengal, as has been pointed out by Arun Joshi. Before him Bal Gangadhar Jambhekar paid attention to this issue and after him reformers like D.K. Karve took it up. Vishnushastri Chiplunkar remained a staunch critic of Lokahitwadi's views, but such criticisms did not deter the latter. For Lokahitwadi ban on widow-remarriage was irrational and inhuman. He was one of the persons to establish Vidhvavivahottejak Mandali in 1863 and helped Vishnushastri Pandit in the formation of Punarvivahottejak Mandali. He even attended the widow-remarriage of Jivkunwar with Lallubhai Mathuradas on August 26, 1872 in Ahmedabad. When some Brahmins of Pune made efforts to make appeal against the Widow Remarriage Act of 1856, Lokahitwadi wrote a powerful article in Gyan Prakash. In 1841 Vishnushastri Bapat in Poona had written a book "Punarvivah Prakaran" on widow-remarriage. It was, however, Lokahitwadi who focused on the issue intensely, and can be called Ishwarchandra Vidyasagar of Maharashtra.[44]

Though Lokahitwadi regarded the British rule in India as "Divine Dispensation" which was beneficial to India, he was an advocate of love for one's own nation. He emphasized that one should do all that was beneficial for one's nation, regard the nation as one's mother and care for its people.[45] He believed that "if some believe that the reform for widow-remarriage should be brought by the British Government (as they have enacted the Sati Abolition Act, they can abolish this evil custom also) they are wrong. It is our custom, so we have to end it. After all, the British are foreigners."[46]

He believed that the way to change was by collective decision. The best way was to form a group of like-minded people. Initially the membership was likely to be small, but gradually it would increase. Once the group was big enough, it would be a community capable of exerting influence and emerging as a reformist force. Such a group, consisting of three to four hundred persons, could bring about consent for a step of social change, and then no one would be able to bring a ban on it. He advocated the need for Hindus to unite on the issue of reform.[47]

Education

Lokahitwadi believed that education was the most important instrument of social change. He believed that the Brahmins were responsible for many of the problems, for they put many obstacles in the path of education, including preventing women from getting access to education, and banning travel abroad, so that people in India were unaware of what was happening in other countries. He urged people to read various new books on new disciplines to widen their horizons.[48] In fact learning meant knowledge of whatever there was in our country as well as in other countries. He advised people to go abroad and thereafter to disseminate the information gained among people to enhance their knowledge.[49] He advised people to discard superstitions and to take up travel to foreign countries.[50] He also argued strongly in favour of learning English.[51]

Eager for the spread of education in our society Lokahitwadi wanted the people to engage in self-study, gain knowledge of the world and to know the authentic history. He believed that one should, after examining all the facts try to seek knowledge about one's own country as well as other countries, and information about ancient as well as contemporary times.[52] He had, evidently, no respect for the Brahmins who were superstitions and followed the Puranas, and said that to follow the words in such books was the cause of the downfall of our society.[53]

Rationality was the guiding star for Lokahitwadi. His ever-inquisitive mind kept him engaged in activities of reading, writing and promotion of education throughout his life. Apart from writing thirty-nine books and editing "Lokahitwadi" (a monthly and quarterly), he played an important role in the formation of Dakshina Fund and Marathi Granthottejak Mandali. He established a library in Wai and was Secretary, Pune Native General Library, and Secretary, Gujarat Vernacular Society, Ahmedabad. He supported efforts to establish a girls' school in Pune and gave the benefit of his experience and ideas to Harkorbai Kanyashala, Ahmedabad as a member of its managing committee, and held fruitful discussions with Mary Carpenter, the British educationist, regarding women's training, when she visited India. He shared Ranade's zeal for propagation of women's education. His wife, two daughters and six daughters-in-law were educated by the standards of those times. Ramabai Ranade wrote, "Rao Saheb Deshmukh and my husband both strongly advocated the cause of women's education. They encouraged their wives to get the women of the place together at least for *haldi-kunku* and read out to them the lives of women like Sita or Savitri and by such efforts persuaded them to educate themselves. They also exhorted us to pay visits to girls' schools to encourage them by giving prizes and such other means." [54]

His arguments in favour of women's education were logical and convincing. According to him, we would remain foolish till we educated our women. It was up to women to teach ways of life to children; if they failed there, there would be no improvement later on.[55]

Lokahitwadi wrote with a refreshing tinge that when widows were educated, they would undoubtedly deal properly with the Pandits. The Brahmins were not in favour of imparting education to women precisely because of this reason. "When women will be educated, they will establish their right."[56] He said the, in our nation, if ten women were learned and also widows, they would have decided to remarry. They would have undoubtedly never stayed in the regime of the wicked Brahmins.[57] "If our women were educated, and if anybody asked them to perform Sati after the husbands' death, they would have caught him by his hair and thrown him! Educated women (if widowed) would remarry and will ask the Shastris why men can marry as many time as they want, while a woman cannot remarry after her husband dies? They will start the scholarly debate and would have given their own interpretations."[58]

Conclusions

Lokahitwadi was involved in many organizations contributing to literary and social organizations, and had established himself as a respected scholar and administrator;

still he found it difficult at times to swim against the current. In spite of being an ardent social reformer and a zealous rationalist, he faltered at times at crucial moments. The discrepancy between his ideas and practice evoked criticisms and ire of progressive elements. In spite of putting his name on the invitation for a widow re-marriage in 1869, he himself could not attend it and invited criticisms of "Indu Prakash" and "Native Opinion". The social boycott because of his strong advocacy of widow-remarriage created a crisis in his family life. His daughter's father-in-law exercised pressure on him to do penance, failure of which would lead to the second marriage of his son-in-law and the consequent miseries of the daughter. His admission later in a letter to Vishnushastri Pandit that in spite of the penance, his views remained unchanged, could not silence his critics. When his own son Krishnarao returned from England after completing his studies as a barrister, due respect was given to religious and social traditions and steps were taken accordingly. In spite of his support for traveling abroad, he himself declined to go to England, when offered an opportunity to go as a witness to the Parliamentary Finance Committee.

M.G. Ranade, Lokahitwadi's friend and close associate, also had to pass through such personal dilemmas. His letter to Lokahitwadi reflected the anguish of the social reformers of those times. He had written, "I know you have family troubles - who has them not? Hence I am with a poor orphan sister, who is kept away from me for months together. My father is sick and I am prevented from going to him by this consideration only, that I might bring troubles on him. This is the lot of us all. We must however stand together for most time to come. Our standing together is our strength and their defeat, and this lesson will bear its fruit."[59] The path of social reformers like Ranade and Lokahitwadi was not easy; it was entangled with personal lives, pressures emanating from them, environment around and their own keen desire to change the society from within. They had to live with constant internal conflicts and overwhelming social pressures.

Lokahitwadi's contribution was significant, as he brought women's issues, especially the issue of widow re-marriage, clearly on the agenda of social reform. He was among the first generation of Indian thinkers who perceived woman as human beings and members of the society and not as mere dependents. Women still had to voice their feelings in their own words. Muktabai, a girl from the backward Mang community, wrote an article in 1855 about the pitiable condition of her community. Tarabai Shinde in her monumental work "Stree-Purush Tulana" (1882) expressed her criticisms against the prevailing patriarchy and prejudices, while Pandita Ramabai's book "Streedharmaniti", published around the same time, contained guide-lines to women's behaviour.

Lokahitwadi's eclectic vision is noteworthy. He did not want to carry the burden of the past in the efforts to reform the society and to better the status of women. According to him, to believe that the arrangement of the past has to be followed for ever was foolishness.[60] His concept of dharma was rooted in rational and human values. His logic was: "did you feed the blind? Did you give clothes to the poor (not Brahmins)? Did you give education to the ignorant? Did you convert evil into good? Did you do good to others? Dharma is based on such issues."[61]

He was one of the earliest thinkers of India, who could see the relation between the social and political issues and identify the link between the progress of a nation and the betterment of women. According to him, if we wanted to promote love and respect for our nation, we would have to eradicate cruel customs like shaving a widow's head and subjecting her to a life of miseries. Banning the Sati system, permitting widow-remarriage and promoting women's education nurture the feeling of love for one's nation.[62] Lokahitwadi's comments on inefficacy of the men in India, in this context, are interesting. He saw the British government as a strong protective husband to the Indians, as the condition of men in our country was the same as that of women in other countries.[63]

Lokahitwadi's persistence on initiating social change by changing the ways of thinking and understanding indicate that he had known the Indian society to its core. He knew that change could not be brought by force. It had to be through understanding. "One cannot run to the government for new laws. People have to understand on their own, and then only they will accept the change."[64]

Lokahitwadi's efforts made in his own way to bring social change remain important. His vision for a better society has not lost its freshness and vitality. His rationality and clarity, his scholarship and sensitiveness, his human values and concern for remarkable for his times, herald the era of social change.

References

1. M.R. Lederle, *Philosophical Trends in Modern Maharashtra*, Popular Prakashan, Bombay, 1976. p.115
2. Ibid, pp 115-6
3. Lokahitwadi, *Lokahitwadinchi Shatpatre* (Marathi),N.R. Inamdar, ed., Continental Prakashan, Pune, 2nd ed. 1960, p.45
4. Arun Joshi, "Lokahitwadikrit Granthasampada", Appendix 1 in *Lokahitwadikrit Nibandhasangraha*, (Marathi), Anant Kakaba Priyolkar, ed., Popular Prakashan, Mumbai, 1996, pp. 587-95; See Appendix 2 for books on Lokahitwadi's life, pp.596-7, Appendix 3 for books on his thought, pp. 598-9 and Appendix 4 for reference books, pp.600-3
5. Arun Joshi, "Lokahitwadi-Gopal Hari Deshmukh" in *Lokahitwadi* (Marathi): Samagra Vangmay I, Govardhan Parikh and Indumati Parikh, eds, Maharashtra Rajya Sahitya Sanskriti Mandal, Mumbai, 1988, p 3
6. N. R. Inamdar. op. cit. letter 108, p. 214
7. Lokahitwadi, "Introduction" (English) to Nigam Prakash (Gujarati), 1874, in *Lokahitwadi: Samagra Vangmay II*, Maharashtra Rajya Sahitya Ani Sanskrity Mandal, Mumbai. 1990, p. 499.
8. N.R. Inamdar, op. cit, letter 70, p. 199
9. Ibid, letter, 100, p. 2
10. Ibid, letter 100, p.3
11. M.R. Lederle, op. cit, p. 115
12. N.R. Inamdar, op. cit, letter 30, pp.185-8

13. Ibid, letter 16, p.198
14. Ibid, letter 70, p.200
15. Lokahitwadi, "Swadhyaya", (Marathi), 1880, in *Lokahitwadi: Samagra Vangmay II*, op. cit., pp. 217-8
16. Lokahitwadi, "An Essay on Female Infanticide" (English), in *Lokahitwadi: Samagra Vangmay I*, op. cit p. 602
17. p. 603
18. "Lokahitwadi", Gyanodaya 15 May 1849, *Lokahitwadi Vangmaya I*, op. cit., pp. 590-2
19. N. R. Inamdar, op. cit. letter 90, p.220
20. Ibid, letter 53, p. 157-8
21. Ibid, Letter 2, p. 217
22. Ibid, letter 15, p. 193
23. Lokahitwadi, Swadhyaya, op. cit, p.289-93
24. N. R. Inamdar, op. cit., letter 15, pp. 191-5
25. Ibid, letter 10, p.189; also letter 104, p. 207
26. Ibid, letter 102, pp. 204-5
27. Lokahitwadi, "Aitihasik Goshti va Upayukta Mahiti", Bhaga II, (Marathi), 1893, *Lokahitwadi Vangmaya I*, op. cit., p. 454
28. N. R. Inamdar op. cit., letter 90, pp. 218-9
29. Ibid, letter 104, p. 208
30. Ibid, letter 104, p. 207
31. Ibid, letter 15, pp. 194-5
32. Swadhyaya, op. cit., pp. 294-7
33. Aryagyanvardhak, (Gujarati), October- December 1884, *Lokahitwadi Vangmaya I*, op. cit., pp. 575-87
34. N. R. Inamdar, op. cit., letter 38, p. 275
35. Ibid, letter 105, p. 211
36. Ibid letter 106, p. 212
37. Ibid, letter 15, p. 195
38. Ibid, letter 70, p. 200
39. Ibid, letter 108, p. 213
40. Ibid, letter 15 p. 194
41. Ibid, letter 104, p. 209
42. *Lokahitwadi Vangmay I*, op. cit., pp. 501-5
43. Gyanprakash, March 3 1856, *Lokahitwadi Vangmay I*, op. cit., pp.497-9
44. Arun Joshi, "Lokahitwadi- Gopal Hari Deshmukh", in *Lokahitwadi Vangmaya I*, op. cit., p. 10
45. N. R. Inamdar, op. cit., letter 67, p. 294
46. Ibid, letter 70, p. 200

47. Ibid, letter 16 p. 196, also letter 99 p. 203
48. Ibid, letter 93, pp. 65-8; letter 95 pp. 68-70
49. Ibid, letter 101, p. 75
50. Ibid, letter 19, p. 17
51. Ibid, letter31, pp.21-5
52. Lokahitwadi, Swadhyaya, op. cit., p 326
53. N. R. Inamdar, op. cit., letter 55, p. 31-2
54. Ramabai Ranade, *Ranade- His wife's Reminiscenes*, Kusumavati Deshpande, translation from Ramabai Ranade's Marathi, Publications Division, Ministry Of Information and Broadcasting, Government of India, New Delhi, 1963, p. 63
55. N. R. Inamdar, op. cit., letter 80, p. 46
56. Ibid, letter 105, p. 211
57. Ibid, letter10, p. 190
58. Ibid, letter 55, p. 32
59. Ananta Kakaba Priyolkar, ed., op. cit., pp. 70-1
60. N. R. Inamdar, letter 106, pp. 211-3
61. Ibid, letter 35, p. 253
62. Swadhyaya, op. cit., Introduction, pp. 156-7
63. Ibid, p. 218
64. N. R. Inamdar, op. cit., letter 7, p. 11

11

Gender Oppression? Female Infanticide among Jadejas of Gujarat

Purabi Ghosh Roy

Gender bias in an extreme and cruel form can be seen in female infanticide practiced by the Jadejas. Infanticide as the practice of killing children while they are still in their infancy is not unknown to human civilization. It is observed that factors such as poverty, famines, war and moral taboos have led people through the ages to kill their infants. But the custom of exclusively and systematically murdering female infants, on the basis of cultural constraints and beliefs, appears to be confined to certain specific groups, including the Rajputs in India[1].

The practice of killing female infants has been prevalent among the Jadejas of Kutch and Kathiawar, Rathore Rajputs of Rajasthan, Rajkumar tribe of Uttar Pradesh and Bengal, Mewatis, a sect of Muslims, whose ancestors were Hindus and among the Lewa Kanbis of Mahikantha in Gujarat. 'The Karada community, chiefly of the Konkan region, also practised female infanticide'[2].

During the medieval period, the practice was no secret. Although the Mughal emperor Jahangir did make a sincere attempt to ban it and some enlightened Indian princes disapproved of it, it had become so much a part of the contemporary socio-religious ethos that to destroy it totally was beyond the capacity of any Indian ruler brought up in a parallel socio-religious contextual framework. The British rulers of India brought with them an entirely variant outlook to social life. Inheriting the Humanistic traditions of the Renaissance, and Protestant Individualism of the Reformation, their framework of the so-called western value structure differed radically from that of the traditional Indians. It was but natural for the colonisers to be morally shocked at this wanton destruction of human life. However, 'colonial masculinity produced a complicity between colonial interests and indigenous orthodoxy'[3]. Moreover, 'colonial masculinity not only discouraged support for reform, but, even more crucially, it underwrote the very protest against social reform. Colonial politics, continued to use social reform as a test of native masculinity – a handy stick with which to beat Indian nationalists'[4].

Of the many disabilities and oppressions to which women in India have been subjected, female infanticide was easily the most cruel and indefensible. Its roots were not necessarily in the cruelty of the Indians as human beings, but more in the oppressiveness of social customs associated with caste, marriage, social hierarchy etc. The existence of the custom of female infanticide was first seriously noted by the British in 1789 among the Rajkumars in the adjoining region of Benaras. Jonathan Duncan, the then English Resident at Benaras happened to discover the practice by accident while conversing with the local zamindars. As Duncan takes care to record, 'the fact was fully authenticated by the evidence and confession of the Rajkumars themselves'[5]. As Duncan wrote in 1808, this custom "is thought to be founded in the Rajkoomar tribe on the inherent extravagant desire of independency entertained by this race of new, joined perhaps, to the necessity of procuring a suitable settlement in marriage for these devoted females were they allowed to grow up, and the disgrace which would ensue from any omission in that respect"[6]. The chronicler went on to state that the only exception which could be brought to notice was this, "that now and then the more wealthy Rajkumars, well sometimes spare and bring up their female issue, especially when they happen to have had none of their male line"[7].

In a letter dated 15th March, 1808, Alexander Walker, the then Resident at Baroda, wrote to the Governor of Bombay that in Kachch and Kathiawar the common expression for infanticide was "Dee Kree marne ne Chal" the custom of killing daughters and "Nanee Dee Kree Marne ne Chal" the custom, of killing young daughters. In conversation and in discussing the subject with the Jadejas, the term used was Dikri Babut, or "the article of girls"[8].

Female infanticide among the Jadejas was first noticed in a Report from Kripa Rama, Minister of the Nawab of Surat, received by Jonathan Duncan, the Governor of Bombay in 1800. "I have heard people say" said the Minister, "that among the tribe of Rajputs and especially among the Rajas of that class, the birth of a daughter in their houses was considered as disgraceful, on which account their women refuse to let their newly born daughters have access to their milk, and put them in any way to death, through all the subdivisions of their tribe, though in several places they do this strong-heartedly kill them"[9]. Kripa Rama received from Gajra Bai, a daughter of a Gaikwad prince of Gujarat, the following Report in February, 1804:

> "Damaji Guicowar carried his arms as far as to Cutch, with the Raja of which a reconciliation took place, on condition that one of the princesses, his daughter, being given in marriage to Damaji, which lady, named Dankur Bye lived among the Guicowars till after Damaji's death, when at her own request, the Raja Fatteh Singh permitted her to return to her own family in Cutch"[10].
>
> "This incidental narrative", says the Minute to the Government, "from Gajra Bye, leading to the question, whether Dankur Bye had, of this marriage any children? It was answered negatively; and Gajra Bye immediately explained that among that lady's caste in Cutch, the

daughters are not brought up, but drowned immediately at their birth in a vessel of milk"[11].

The custom of female infanticide clearly had no religious sanction. The act committed privately could not be detected for a long time because the perpetrators of the crime took care not to be detected. It was argued that the practice commenced because Raja Jada was unable to get a suitable match for his daughters. "Raja Jada who sent his Rajguru to find a suitable match for his daughter, but not finding one, he advised the Raja to kill his daughter"[12]. Raja Jada was aware of the heinousness of the act which his priest or Rajguru had advised him to commit, "but the Rajguru at length removed the Raja's scruples, by consenting to load himself with the guilt, and to become in his own person responsible for all the consequences of the sin"[13]. From that time it is believed that the Jadejas began the practice of female infanticide. However, this sounds like a child's tale. "The story though clumsy and inelegant in the invention connects the origin of infanticide, with high rank, Brahmin authority and remote antiquity"[14].

The British Resident at Baroda, Colonel Alexander Walkers report shows that the Jadejas' original home was in Sindh. After the Muslim conquest of Sindh, Jadejas migrated to Kachch where they established themselves and retained their own religion. According to James Tod, the Jadejas had also "conceived many peculiar notions of their superiority and they undervalued and despised the tribes amongst whom they had obtained a compulsory settlement"[15]. Walker's Report demonstrates that the Rajputs with their traditional sense of pride believed in the purity of their bloodline. Moreover, the Rajputs of different states vied with each other in claiming social superiority and higher status. Jadeja Rajputs in Kathiawar claimed superiority over all other clans of Rajputs. Enthoven has observed that clan as such was endogamous. 'Except relatives there are none of their own tribe'[16]. Further, "Poverty does not lower a Rajput's social position. But his position is injured if he married a woman who is not a Rajput. He also lowers himself if he marries his daughter to someone who is socially his own inferior"[17]. Enthoven observed that the name of a daughter given in marriage to a boy of a lower status was not entered by the genealogist in the family list. "Daughters married into a family of inferior birth are not entitled to any special honour at any family gathering or feast"[18].

Tod analysed that although religion nowhere sanctioned the practice of infanticide the laws which regulated their marriage promoted infanticide. "Not only is inter marriage prohibited between families of the same clan (Kul) but between those of the same tribe (Gotra); and though centuries may have intervened, since their separation, and branches thus transplanted may have lost their original patronymic, they can never be regrafted on the original system"[19].

The matrimonial market for a bridegroom had narrowed. Marriage for girls was compulsory among the Hindus. In Gujarat there is a proverb that 'an old man may die unmarried but an old woman cannot do so' – "Doso Kunvaro mare par Doshi Kunwari na mare"[20]. "... It is an established custom that a female may not marry into any caste or tribe which is not at least of equal rank with her own. To marry an inferior in their eyes, is degradation, but to remain unmarried is actual dishonour"[21]. Jadejas admitted the practice themselves.

These material facts, however, were garbed in a religious cloak. According to Hindu belief, it was a son and a son alone, who could perform the rites for liberation of the ancestors, from the cycle of life and death. A son was not only a material inheritor, but also a spiritual one. The birth of a son opened, so it was believed, the gates of heaven to his parents. A daughter was a spiritual liability and not an asset.

Walker's Report corroborates that the Jadejas were not willing at first to speak on the "Dee Kree Marne ne Chal", remarking that it was private affair of the women. It was found out however that it was very much an affair of the men, as it was according to their express orders that the crime was perpetrated by the women. Their reluctance to acknowledge the crime was partly due to the commonly accepted religious belief that killing a child was a heinous crime.

Some of the men of the Jadeja community said that if they reared their daughters, they might perhaps be guilty of wrong conduct and bring disgrace to the family. And also it was the first duty of a Hindu father to provide a suitable husband for his daughter and it was reproachful that "they should pass the age of puberty without having been affianced and be under the necessity of living in a state of celibacy"[22]. Another significant factor was that intercaste marriage was not allowed between families of the same tribe. The disquieting element was that the killing of a girl child was also conceptually viable from an economic standpoint in such a socio-cultural structure.

From a study of different motives which made the Jadejas kill their female offspring, one may state that the root cause of this social custom can be found in their peculiar institutions of caste and marriage. In patriarchal ideology the chastity and purity of woman is emphasised. For it was feared that '... Its erosion would lead to the loss of female honour, growth of half-castes and the destruction of ancestral rites'[23]. In a hierarchical society like India purity of caste was maintained through women. "The principal objective of the girl's male kinsfolk was, and still is, to ensure that their own status will be enhanced by giving her in marriage in a condition of great natural purity to a high ranking spouse"[24]. Disgrace was attached to marriage with a man of inferior rank. "Since a patriarchal social order is based on the control of female sexuality, inter-sex relationship was prohibited and deeply hierachised"[25]. "Pratiloma is tabooed because it runs contrary to existing social arrangements based on patrilineal descent, patrilocality, and male authority. In a pratiloma marriage, the wife cannot live with her natal relatives since her children are of lower ritual status. She can move into her husband's partrilineage but as a member of a superior caste, she would upset the hierarchies of domestic relations based on male dominance and female subordination"[26].

Vanity, ignorance, pride, avarice, the cares of a family, the disgrace that would attend the misconduct of their women, the difficulty of establishing them in life and apprehension of exposing their daughters to ill treatment were the different causes that induced the Jadejas to commit infanticide[27].

Another vital reason given for this practice was the high degree of expense incurred in providing husbands for their daughters. The dowry system was in a way corollary to the hypergamic marriage system, which forbade a woman of a particular caste to marry a man belonging to a social status lower then her own. A boy's father was always considered superior to a girl's father. Some of the men of the Jadeja community believed that if they reared heir daughters they would bring disgrace to the family. The emphasis in the patriarchal group was in the male progeny. In a gender segregated purdah society, a woman became a non-being, "a variable entity whose own lineage was an erasable line. She (rather her baby) served as a vehicle for the continuity of the male lineage"[28]. In fact, this function or role was her sole justification.

The history of female infanticide presents a sordid reading. Its roots were not necessarily in the cruelty of any particular group as human beings, but more in the cruel oppression of many social customs associated with caste, marriage, social hierarchy etc. Walker reported that the Jadejas worshipped the Goddess Ashapuri (The Hope-Fulfilled), whose principal shrine was in Kachch. In Hindu tradition a Goddess is often addressed as Mother. The 'Mother' image is dominant in Indian thought. "The concept of adya shakti, primal or original power, is entirely feminine in India. It is the male principal in the godhead, Purusha, that is reliable but relatively passive, weak, distant and secondary. That is why the deities that preside over those critical sectors of life which one cannot control - such as the success of crops and the occurrence of famines (food), protection against cholera and small pox (personal survival), and child birth and child health (perpetuation of race) – are all mother figures"[29].

A Jadeja considered the death of a daughter as 'an infallible consequence'[30] after its birth, and her birth was considered to be an event of such insignificance that he was seldom apprized of it. To render this deed, the mother was generally the executioner of her own daughter. This maternal neglect, according to Ashis Nandy, "is a weird expression of woman's hostility towards womanhood and also, symbolically, toward her own self. This classic instance of the psychological defense of turning against self by identifying with the aggressive male draws attention to the way in which some social institutions have made woman herself, a participant in her self-repudiation and intra-aggression"[31]. Moreover, in a patriarchal culture, blaming women was a convenient defence mechanism for men.

Unfortunately, the practice of female infanticide still persists. It has been observed that a community called Kallars in the Madurai region of Tamil Nadu practiced female infanticide in the recent past. It is interesting to note that the circumstances that forced Jadejas to kill their daughters are still in existence. Marriage expenses are still enormous. A daughter is an economic drain, and a socio-economic liability.

S. Krishnaswamy points out commonalties between the Kallars of Tamil Nadu and the Rajputs of western India. He opined, "During certain periods of history members of both Kallars and Rajputs were seen as rulers in certain small pockets. Whereas Rajputs continued their traditional occupation as warriors even during the medieval period, Kallars ceased to be so"[32]. Kallars, original a warrior clan, were known for their military valour. The declining sex ratio clearly indicates the inferior status of women. Today we come across foeticide cases – amniocentesis or the practice of sex determination of a child with a view to aborting female foetuses. Thus, female infanticide has taken a new dimension in the shape of female foeticide.

Indian woman is still not in position to avail of the opportunities provided by the Indian Constitution. For instance the Dowry Prohibition Act was passed in 1961, and amended in 1984. Despite legislation, dowry continues to be demanded and given. Vibhuti Patel suspects that researches could even today find cases of female infanticide in various parts of India. She posits, "is it really better to be born and left to die than to be killed as foetus?"[33]. She wonders whether the birth of lakhs of unwanted female children would improve the status of women. The worst aspect of amniocentesis is, "it is practised by all, irrespective of their class, caste, religion, educational and cultural background, while female infanticide was limited only among certain castes"[34].

References

1. Selections from the Records of the Bombay Government, No. XXXVII – New Series, Part II, pp. 19-20.
2. Edward Moor, *Hindu Infanticide*, London, Johnson & Co. 1811, p.105
3. Mrinalini Sinha, *Colonial Masculinity: The 'manly Englishman' and the 'effeminate Bengali' in the late nineteenth century*, New Delhi, Kali for Women, 1997. p. 142
4. Ibid.
5. Political Department, Vol. 24 of 1854, East India Affairs, p. 22.
6. Ibid.
7. John Wilson, *History of the Suppression of Infanticide in Western India*, Bombay, Smith Taylor & Co. 1855, p. 4.
8. Secret and Political Department, Diary No 228/1808, History of Infanticide, p.3962.
9. J. Peggs, *Female Infanticide*, London, 1828, p. 27.
10. Ibid.
11. Ibid.
12. Selections from the Records of the Bombay Government – Part II, Op. cit., p. 6
13. Ibid. p 5.
14. John Cormack, *Account of the Abolition of Female Infanticide in Guzerat,* Bombay, Black, Parry & Co. 1855, pp. 27–28.
15. Selections from the Records of the Bombay Government, Part II, Op cit., p.6.
16. Edward Moor, Op cit., p. 34
17. R.E. Enthoven, *The Tribes and Castes of Bombay*, Vol. III, Bombay, Government Central Press, 1922, p. 275.
18. Ibid., p. 276.
19. James Tod, *Annals and Antiquities of Rajasthan*, Vol. II, London, Oxford University Press, 1920, p. 743.
20. Neera Desai, *Social Change in Gujarat*, Bombay, Vora, 1978, p.66.
21. John Cave-Browne, *Indian Infanticide: Its Origin, Progress and Repression*, London, 1857, p. 9

22. Secret and Political Department Diary No. 228/1808 Op.cit., p. 3944.
23. Tanika Sarkar, *Hindu wife, Hindu nation: Community, Religion And Cultural Nationalism*, New Delhi, Permanent Black, 2001 p. 208.
24. Michael Allen 'The Hindu View of Women' in Michael Allen and S.N. Mukherjee, eds, *Women in India and Nepal, Monographs on South Asia* No. 8, ANU, 1982, p.6.
25. Kamala Ganesh, 'Seclusion of Women and the Structure of Caste', in Maithreyi Krishna Raj and Karuna Chenana, eds, *Gender and The Household Domain: Social and Cultural Dimension*, New Delhi, Sage, 1989, p.89.
26. Ibid.
27. Selections from the Records of the Bombay Government No. XXXVII, Part II, p. 19.
28. Manushi, Member 71, July – August, 1992, p.15.
29. Ashis Nandy, 'Woman Verses Womanliness in India: An Essay in Social and Political Ideology', in Rehana Ghadially, ed, *Women in Indian Society,* New Delhi, Sage, pp. 72-73
30. See Edward Moor, Op. cit., pp. 57-58
31. Ashis Nandy, Op. cit., p. 71
32. S. Krishnaswamy, 'Female Infanticide in Contemporary India: A Case Study of Kallars in Tamil Nadu', in Ghadially, ed, Op. cit., p 188.
33. Vibhuti Patel, 'Sex Determination and Sex Preselection Tests: Abuse of Advanced Technologies', in Ghadially, ed., Ibid., p. 182.
34. Ibid.

12

Jain Women's Urge for Education: A Gender Perspective

Padmaja A. Patil

British Rule in India brought in its wake a uniform administration, Western education and modern means of communications. All these factors contributed to a general awakening among all castes and creeds of Indian people to an extent unparalleled in the history of India. Socio-religious and intellectual awakening may be traced in all castes and sections of the society in a varying degree during the British period. So also, there emerged awareness among the Jains of their backwardness and the need for education in general and female education in particular. The paper is an attempt to understand the views of the Jain women about education and their gender perspective.

During the British regime, Sindh, Gujarat, Maharashtra and South Maharashtra were four administrative divisions of Bombay Presidency[1]. Kolhapur and Sangli were princely states under the control of Bhosales of Kolhapur and the Patwardhans respectively. By the end of the 19th century, the Jain population both in urban and rural areas was mainly concentrated in Sangli-Kolhapur states, in Belgaum, Dharwad and Solapur districts. The majority of them belonged to *Digambar* sect of the Jains. They were engaged in agriculture, resided in villages and were not economically well off. But those who resided in the urban areas and were engaged in mercantile activities were quite well-to-do[2]. In Kolhapur the Jains resided mainly in the rural area. As such, the Jain community in the region of Kolhapur remained backward in comparison to the Jain community in other regions, especially their north Indian counterparts. In 1901, Jains formed about 4.55 percent of the total population of the State. However, where the literary percentage of the community is concerned, only 37 males out of 20,199 in Kolhapur State were acquainted with the English languages as per the census report for the year 1881. Only one lady, Godubai Upadhye could read and write and there was not a single Jain female in Kolhapur State who had learnt English.[4] The Jain women formed about 48.55 percent of the total population of this community.[5] The low literacy rate of the Jain community may be traced to certain geographical and economic causes and also to certain deep rooted social practices and customs. In Jain philosophical and religious systems, women enjoy a greater degree of liberty and freedom. In Jain *'Darshanas'*, religious books, the soul of male and female is identical. But in reality women were unfortunate victims conservative attitude of the social orthodoxy and conservative of the Jain community. It looked down upon educating its women folk. Educating a women meant calling the divine curse on the family. This was the general sentiment in the society.[6] In cities like Bombay and Poona, the Jain men were influenced by Western ideas and wanted to educate the Jains in general.

Efforts for the Development of Education

The British rule broadened the base of education in India, especially, in the princely State of Kolahapur by starting a strong movement of social change in the last decade of 19th century by Chhatrapati Shahu Maharaj (1894-1922). In his efforts, he followed Mahatma Jotiba Phule. Social welfare of the non-Brahmin backward communities was the aim of this movement. Chh. Shahu was the backbone of all the social movements. The major impact of the social movement was felt in the area of progress in educational field. And the doors for education were opened to all the communities. Thus major changes occurred in the field of education of the State of Kolhapur.[7]

Many social workers were bold enough to express their views openly and publicly. As awakening precedes any reform, an attempt was made to trace the same in the Jain community. Prominent persons like Adiraj Devendra Upadhye and Anna Babaji Latthe, (Kolhapur), Anna Phadyappa Chougule, (Belgaum), Manikchand Hirachand Jhaveri (Bombay), Sheth Hirachand Nemachand Doshi, (Solapur) gave thought to it. These social workers established Dakshin Bharat Jain Sabha for the upliftment of Jains for socio-religious and educational progress of Jain community. General awakening among the Jain Community was at a rather slow pace and still going slower in the promotion of female education. The promoters had to cross a number of obstacles right from the elimination of the deep rooted social evils such as child marriage, widow problems, and low status of women in household affairs. To improve the educational condition and to make them aware, special efforts were made in all possible directions for promotion of female education by individuals, by the government, by the Jain press, by spreading the cultural thoughts and ideas of Jain intellectuals and social workers.[8]

Jain Women's Views About Education

Seth Hirachand Nemachand Doshi, an eminent social worker was educated at Bombay and was associated with Jain community of Kolhapur. He published a periodical "*Jain Bodhak*", at Solapur in 1885.[9] Many articles stressing on female education were published in its issues. The thoughts of scholars and learned men regarding women's education were published. Special efforts were made to inspire the women to take modern education. Amongst many others, Jains of Kolhapur were the regular readers of the '*Jain Bodhak*'. The influence of such article can well be judged. A certain person wrote an article on 'women's education' in the issue No. 135-136, year 12th, Nov.-Dec, 1869. His name was Adiraj Devendra Upadhye.[10] He was husband of Godubai Upadhaye. An anonymous Jain woman was so inspired by it that she wrote a letter to the editor Hirachand Nemachand Doshi, in response to above mentioned article about women's education. She gave vent to her suppressed thoughts which were common to hundreds of Jain women. This was published in the issue of February, 1987.[11]

While soliciting to publish the later she says, "consider my article in the same way as I am offering '*Tilgul of makarsankranti*' to my brother". Further she writes, "I understand that educating women has lot of advantages. But it is very sad to that my Jain brothers are least interested in the women's education, which I consider very unfortunate. We are discouraged as both our parents and parents-in-laws think that there is no point in educating, which I consider very unfortunate. We are discouraged as both of our parents and parents-in-laws think there is no point in educating girls, as ultimately they have to manage the house-bold after marriage. After marriage the husbands' house practically follows the same views. They are not paying any attention to the education. Getting a progressive minded husband is almost one in a million and perhaps which is not the fate of common women. When our own men are not aware of the values of education, how can they help their women folk in this respect. In spite of this, if any man wants to educate his wife he is afraid of social taboos being observed generation after generation. If you want to take the bold step of educating women, you should encourage them by offering scholarships and other facilities. Other castes and communities established scholarships and other facilities. Other castes and communities established women's associations like Women's Association of Bombay, and have surged far ahead in this respect. Shri Saraswati Mandir of Solapur and *Khajagi Stree Parikshak Mandal*, Pune are but a few examples. They are far ahead in this race whereas we Jains are still not woken up. You are expressing socio-religious views in your weekly, but, I feel, your must start a daily Jain newspaper for women only."

Another important document is the resolution by the Jain Women for the spread of Jain Women's Education in the year 1899. Colonial rules set the change in motion. Indians reshaped the imported ideas and institutions to fit the social and cultural milieu. The ideology that emerged to redefine gender relations was an amalgam of new western ideas, indigenous concepts and the response of Indian men and women to the western presence in their midst. The first generation of Western educated young men evoked reason as the touchstone for both the ideas and action. Educated young among the Jains like A. B. Latthe, A. P. Chougule and others tried to establish an institution for the progressive Jains in Southern Maharashtra at Stawanidhi (Nipani), now in Karnataka State, on 3rd April 1899.[12] In its first meeting Godubai Upadhaye boldly moved a resolution.[13]

"We unfortunate women have gathered here for taking steps to improve our status in society though education. Seeing this gathering I am very much hopeful and happy and therefore I want to put forward a resolution: 'Man and woman are considered to be the left and right side of a social human being. One is incomplete without the other. In such a society when the other half (that is woman) is uneducated, it does not make a whole a whole and complete healthy picture, one side is paralyzed. Whose wives are uneducated will not be able to progress and will lag behind in the race for progress. So it is necessary to develop education in our women.' In our literature, we can get references of Anantmati and Chetanadevi being educated. Kings in ancient India appointed special tutors for their daughters and wives. But during Mughal period, this tradition stopped and this dark period for women continued till today. Men fear that, if their women were educated, they will be dominated and this gave rise to an inferiority complex. But this is not so, because both are two sides of the same coin, and woman is also a partner in his progress. In many instances, it is the educated woman who has proved more valuable than the educated man. This is main reason for putting forward this resolution of women's education."

Critical Aalysis of Jain Women Views About Gender Perspectives and Historical Facts

The two above-mentioned documents represent the views of Jain women about their status, condition, educational backwardness and gender perspective. While analyzing these two documents it can be concluded that Godubai Upadhye appears highly enlightened in her thoughts. Irrespective of her lack of formal education. Marathi language of this document is very lucid and effective. Though the 19th century was the century of enlightenment about women problems, there were so many social taboos and restrictions which prevented women from getting education. Even to present such a resolution was considered as a very bold step in the then Jain community in Kolhapur region. But, nevertheless, we come across their view, their urge for education and, of course, gender perspective, as expressed in these documents.

First of all they pinpointed that the pitiable condition of Jain women was due to their men folk. They neglected woman's education because of social taboos at her father's and husband's house. Godubai has given serious thought to the problems of not educating Jain women. According to her, Jain men-folk were less interested in women's education, as they themselves were unaware about the values of education. Parents' approach was that there was no use educating girls because their future was limited to house-hold work after marriage. For this she directly blames narrow-mindedness of menfolk.

She felt that the husband should take interest in the matter of education but such a husband is rare and it is still rarer to be in her fate. She remarked, "Our education will be possible only when husband takes car of it. But getting such kind of progressive minded husband is one in a million and whether that one will be in our luck." Her expression clearly reflected her gender and feminist perspective. But she openly criticized and expressed her feelings without any reservation or fear.

Further she pointed out that eminent Jain male writers never paid proper attention to the women's point of view and her compulsions in their writings. In these documents women not only blamed their men-folk for their situation but also suggested some ways for coming out of it. She says, "We must take bold steps by encouraging and offering them scholarships and other facilities for education." While comparing position of Jain women with the women of other castes and communities she observed, "Other castes and communities have established their association and have gone far ahead in this respect like Women Association in Bombay, Shri Saraswati Mandir of Solapur and Khajagi Stree Parikshak Mandali, Pune. Eminent scholars and donors of Jain community must start schools for us and for nation's sake."

Lastly, she suggested that the 'daily' newspapers would be more beneficial than 'monthly' magazines, because dailies could put forth everyday problems of women and also explain their rights. The Jains were now waking up in this respect were. Therefore, the daily women's newspaper may serve the purpose. They have stated with conviction that the educated men and uneducated women in the Jain community presented a somewhat distorted picture of the society which hampered the progress. Jain men-folk feared that if women were to be educated they would not behave submissively. They would act with superiority complex. But this was a false fear because in many instances it was the educated women who proved more valuable than an educated man.

Considering these views it can be stated that they were able to suggest ways and means of coming out of this backward situation by providing gender equality without suffering from inferiority complex. These documents also show that, the women knew the sequence of historical events which prevented them from taking education in mediaeval India. There is a very important sentence by Godubai Upadhaye which demands critical analysis of the past.[14] "In ancient India women were taught at home but during Mughal period, this tradition stopped and this dark period for women continued till today."

Taking into consideration of Godubai Upadhye's statement who was living in princely state of Kolhapur, here I want to draw the attention to the impact of Maratha war of Independence on the common man. After Chh. Shivaji's death, Aurangzeb came to Deccan in 1682. His aim was to annihilate the Maratha power with an excuse to chase his son Akbar who had revolted against him. The campaign ended with his death in 1707. At that time Maharani Tarabai of Kolhapur was leading the Marathas.[15] Tarabai established seat of Maratha power at the fort Panhala and fought against Aurangzeb. Tarabai, after consolidating the Maratha army at Panhala fort, fought the Mughal army bravely. It is said that almost one lakh soldiers of the Mughal army had surrounded the region around Panhala. This created feeling of terror and depression the region around Panhala.[16] Their morale was at lowest ebb. And hence they had to remain behind closed doors, due to the fear of the enemy. The Jain women were no exception to this. Since then, it became a common practice with Jain mercantile community to keep their women in closed enclaves.

Conclusion

It can be concluded that there was a fear in the minds of common women which was reflected in writings of Godubai and other. During the war of independence of 27 years, it was prime necessity to protect the women-folk from Mughal forces. This was the view of Godubai Upadhye, which prevented her from taking education. We cannot blame or criticize her because her views and understanding represented common feelings during that time.

Finally, I would like to state that for the first time these document are discussed here. They can now be used for the reconstruction of the regional socio-religious history of Southern Maharashtra. Through these documents we get a fair picture of Jain women's gender feelings and the urge of self-development through modern education. The major thrust areas for reform were caste and gender inequalities, which reigned supreme during the last decade of the 19th century. The thoughts represented by Godubai and an unknown woman, are representative of the general feelings of contemporary unknown woman, are representative of the general feelings of contemporary women-folk, irrespective of caste and creed.

Godubai Upadhye's contribution lies in the fact that she brought to the limelight the need for educating Jain women. Her thoughts about Mughal emperors and its linking with Jain males and their attitude towards women provided a mere excuse. It can be concluded that her opinion was based on a very limited experience and exposure.

References

1. Padmaja Patil, *Annasaheb Lathhe and His Times,"* unpublished thesis, submitted to Shivaji University, Kolhapur, 1986, p. 34.
2. Vilas Sangave, (1975), *"Dakshin Bharat Jain Sabhecha Itihas."* P. 21.
3. Census of Kolhapur State, 1901, Vide Sangave Op. Cit., p. 13.
4. Census of Kolhapur State, 1891, Vide Sangave Op. Cit., p. 30.
5. *Maharashtra State Gazetteers*, Kolhapur District Gazetteer, "There people and their culture," Bombay Govt. Central Press, 1960, p 105.
6. Pandurang Kale, *"Karmayogini Shrimati, Kalantrei"*, Bombay, (1976), pp. 12-13.
7. A. B. Latthe, *"Memoirs of H. H. Chh. Shahu Maharaja of Kolhapur,"* Vol. II p 448.
8. S. S. Chougule, *"Jain Samajache Kartabgar Divangat Nete,"* (1988), introduction and p. 66.
9. Bramhachari Shital Prasadaji, Danvir Manikchand, Surat (1919), p. 215.
10. Ibid, *"Jain Bodhak,"* Nov-Dec., 1896.
11. *"Jain Bodhak,"* Feb. 1897, pp. 1-5.
12. Padmaja Patil, Op.Cit., p 34.
13. *"Jain Bodhak,"* issue 5th to 8th, March to June 1899, pp. 15-17.
14. Ibid.
15. G.S. Sardesai, *New History of the Marathas*, Vol I., Pune, 1936, p. 307; *Maharashtra State Gazetteers*, Maratha Period, Govt. of Maharashtra, Bombay, 1967, p. 31
16. Brij Kishore, *Tarabai and her times*, Asia Publishing House, Bombay, 1963, pp. 69-79; Shalini Patil, *Maharani Tarabai of Kolhapur*, S. Chand & Company, New Delhi, 1987, pp. 90-93.

13

A Critical Review of Historiography with Special Reference to Women's Health Care

Meherjyoti Sangle

Women all over the world belong to the subordinate section of the societies concerned. Therefore they do not get a place in history, which normally records the life and achievements of privileged groups. The Indian scenario is slightly different in the sense that women of early India got some space in mainstream history. However, the context was in response to the criticism of women's condition in Indian society by the missionaries and colonial administrators. The purpose was to highlight the status of women in early India and thereby support the agenda of social reform.

In the mid-seventies of the last century the history of women got strong encouragement from the publication of *Toward Equality*[1] report on the condition of Indian women. In fact, the second wave of Feminism made its impact on educated Indian women also. They criticized the mainstream Indian historiography in which women got very little place. They also pointed out its androcentric bias. During the last decade feminist historians have explored fresh and unconventional areas to document women's experiences and achievements.

Thus there is now substantial literature on the history of Indian women.

Nevertheless, some areas of central concern to women still remain altogether uncovered or covered very little. One such area, which is of our special interest, is women's health care. The purpose of the present paper is to briefly survey the available historiography on women and highlight how much coverage this problem of health care has received, the nature and content of research in the field as also its methods and procedures of collecting and interpreting the data. For the purposes of convenience therefore, the paper is divided into four sections.

The first is devoted to features of precolonial and post-colonial works on women's history that belong to traditional school of historiography. The second is devoted to books conceived in feminist perspective. The third section is specifically devoted to books on history of health and medicine in general. The concluding section focuses on some very recent works that devote large space to women's health care.

I

As pointed out above, historiography on women in India began in the context of the social reform movement of nineteenth century. It matured into the national approach to Indian history and its representative book is A.S. Altekar's *The Position of Women in Hindu Civilization.*[2] Though published in pre-Independence time, it has exercised great influence on post-Independence publications as well. It surveys the position of Hindu women from Vedic period to our own times and views them in familial roles. Uma Chakravarti has done a critical evaluation of Altekar's book. Her perceptive comment is "Altekar's work represents the best that is available to us by way of women's studies in history but it also shows us very sharply the limitations of the traditional approach."[3] She pleaded for adopting a feminist approach to rewriting the past of Indian women. After pointing out the man-centered perspective in Altekar's work she says, "There thus is an urgent need to move forward and rewrite history, a history that does justice to women, by examining social processes and the structures they create, thus critically shaping and conditioning the relations between men and women. Just as Altekar displaced Mill in his work, it is time we realized that despite Altekar's substantial contribution we must lay his ghost aside and begin afresh."[4]

Yet another kind of writing which came out of the nationalist approach was in the nature of "contributory history." The authors identified women considered great in Indian mythology and history and described virtues and achievements of each in the form of a biographical sketch. This is technically termed "contributory history" that describes women's contribution to their status and their oppression by male-defined society.[5] To this category belong Swami Madhavananda and R.C. Majumdar's *Great Women of India*[6], Padmini Sengupta's *The Story of Women in India*[7], *Dictionary of National Biography* edited by S.P. Sen[8] and *Women of India*[9] edited by Tara Ali Baig and others. All these works and others of their type continue the traditional view of treating women of the past in narrative pattern. There is hardly any new framework. So much idealized is the representation of women in these works that hardly any real woman emerges from them. Women have been viewed in male-defined roles. Given this attitude, it is futile to expect any author of being concerned with problems of women's health. One could name and summarize the contents of many more books of this school without locating any new features other than those noted above.

What surprises one is the fact that the hold of this approach continues well into 21st century. Indra Gupta's book *India's 50 Most Illustrious women*[10] from the very title indicates how a section of historians is unable to shake off traditional approach to history writing. The book contains fifty biographical sketches of Indian women of the nineteenth and twentieth centuries who distinguished themselves in a variety of fields. The criteria of selection was participation in freedom movement and social reform and contribution of various fields like literature, art, music, dance, cinema, sports and adventure or winning of recognition with awards, the highest being Bharat Ratna.

The problem appears to be that the Annales or Subaltern schools of historiography have hardly proved strong enough to discourage a section of historians from moving away from the approach of documenting the lives of only heroes and heroines. The concept of people's history or 'total history' has a long way to go.

II

Coming now to the origin and development of feminist perspective on women's history in India, we could well begin with its ideological origins. Gerda Lerner, a pioneer in the field, thus proclaimed its birth,

> "The emergence of feminist consciousness as a historical phenomenon is an essential part of the history of women."[11]

Verily feminism is an ideology that brought 'women to history and history to women'. In view of the fact that all history recorded achievements and activities of men only, even the idea that 'women have a history' and 'women are in history' appeared revolutionary. Such a history was to begin with searching answers to certain questions like,

> "Who are the women missing from history? Who are the women of achievement and what did they achieve?.....The history of notable women is the history of the exceptional, even deviant women and does not describe mass of women..... Women of different classes have different historical experiences."[12]

This was something like accepting a challenge, in the sense that no history is possible without source material and women being a subordinate group had no hand in creating it.

On the Indian scene we need to note that feminist ideology and its perspective on history was to develop only after the publication of the *Foward Equality* [13] report in 1974. Under a directive from the U.N.O., the Government of India appointed a committee to study the condition of Indian women at all levels, upper as well as lower. This report gave an overall picture of women's condition in India. It highlighted the fact that condition of women in postcolonial India not much different from the one in colonial India even though they had participated in freedom struggle. The influence of this report on history writing was great. Lives of ordinary women attracted as much attention of historians as those of great women.

However, much earlier to this was published a work not conceived in feminist terms and yet breaking away from the framework of traditional history of women. Neera Desai's *Women in Modern India*[14] is the first book of social history of Indian women by a woman. Even for the premodern period, which is treated as background, she offered new angles to interpret the facts. She discussed a wide range of topics, tracing the ways and phases through which women stepped out of traditional roles to modernized ones. In the context of various socio-religious and political movements she located the areas that offered opportunity and encouragement to women for participation in public spheres.

Another work that could be considered here is Alfred de'Souza's *Women in Contemporary India: Traditional Images and Changing Roles.*[15] It is a collection of articles in which some focus on regional variations, some bring out various roles played by women in society, the legal and constitutional rights accorded to them. Here also there is an effort to trace changing images of women from 'traditional' to 'modern' ones.

By far the most important contribution in the field is by Geraldine Forbes *Women in Modern India.*[16] It is remarkable in terms of clear conceptual framework and methodology. It covers women under colonial rule and in post-colonial India. Beginning with the social reform that was initiated by men to educate Indian women, it shows how the spread of education worked change in women. She discusses different organizations of women and various movements to achieve women's rights. The work is as much factual as analytical and thus represents refreshing change in the trend of writing.

Among the anthologies that focus on the birth of modern India and contribution of women therein we have to note *Women Pioneers in India's Renaissance,*[17] edited by Sushila Nayer and Kamla Mankekar. The title reflects the nature of its content. It is a collection of sixty seven articles dealing with significant contribution of women in fields ranging from freedom struggle and women's liberation on the one hand to society and culture on the other. The book also brings home how women pioneers enriched lives of other women and helped in the shaping of modern India. One also gets a glimpse into their struggles, hopes, aspirations and achievements. The value of volume is enhanced by the photographs that have been added with life sketches.

Yet another collection, but with a different form, is also worthy of note. *Women Images* [18] by Pratibha Jain and Rajan Mohan is primarily concerned with multiplicity of women's images in Indian art, literature as also in classical and folk traditions. It provides a conceptual analysis and offers valuable insights into a variety of issues pertaining to representation of women. On the whole, the collection fulfils its purpose by offering an objective understanding of visions and ideas about Indian women.

Before closing this section we need to consider two more collections which brought a turning point in historical writing about Indian women. The first one, entitled *Recasting Women: Essays in Colonial History*[19] edited by Kumkum Sangari and Sudesh Vaid breaks away from the narrative model of history and adopts a critical and analytical approach with feminist perspective.

It consists of thirteen articles, some of which are devoted to micro study of women of a region while others give a critique of historiography in a given field and bring out in the process the changing nature of patriarchy. The other anthology, *Women and Culture*[20] also edited by Kumkum Sangari and Sudesh Vaid, contains seventeen articles and, as reflected in the title, focuses on cultural history. Most articles offer empirical data on a theme, which then is critically analyzed in the light of feminist concepts and theories. The traditional images of Indian women as derived from art, literature and mythology of different cultures as also from films and political movements are analyzed from feminist perspective.

It might be clear from this rather hurried survey of books inspired by feminist ideology that most writers have been concerned with preparing a critique of traditional historiography, while a section of historians is concerned with deconstructing traditional images. No doubt, many more books of this school remain uncovered but paucity of space does not permit citing and commenting on them. In any case, the representative selection given here, as in the preceding section, clearly shows that women's Health Care has not attracted attention of any of the historians of this school as well.

III

This utter lack of historical literature on the health of women is difficult to explain. Historians, whether of traditional or feminist school, have discussed endlessly the customs of child marriage, *purdah*, sati, denial of education, and enforced widowhood without ever contemplating how these customs must have affected women's health. Again, the value of women as baby producing machines must have resulted in high rates of maternal mortality in the absence of proper medical care, but this tragic fact of history has failed to motivate any historian to undertake research even for colonial India, for which sources must be available. Apart from customs and general attitude of exploiting women's reproductive capacity, there were rituals and superstitions affecting physical and psychological health of women. Taken as a whole, the subject of research naturally becomes vast and varied but it is yet to interest even women historians.

Apart from customs and superstitions affecting women's health adversely, ignorance of women about their health problems must be taken as major factor. With denial of formal education for women, awareness about medical care among them is futile to expect. Added to this must have been malnutrition, restriction on free movement, dislike of the girl-child, and denial of proper baby-care, making their lives miserable, perhaps unbearable.

For the past couple of decades history of Health and Medicine has emerged as a potential area of research and we intend to survey some books in this section, focusing in general on the field. By its very nature the area requires an interdisciplinary approach, in which inter-linking of a number of factors, such as environment, climate, administrative policies, ideology of racism, nature of diseases and plurality of medicines, epidemics, vaccinations and their impact, reaction and response of the natives and so on, need to be taken into consideration. Finally, though the field is purely scientific, the interpretation of the data has varied according to the schools of historian belong to Orientalist, Imperialist and Marxist, Feminist or Postmodernist.

Before coming to the Indian scenario, it will be helpful to survey the nature and content of some studies in the West. We could begin with the thesis entitled *Medical Women: A Thesis and A History*[21] by Sophia Jex-Blake. It gives a detailed idea of hurdles of medical practice by women and also history of the movement in England. This includes the story of the struggle for the women's medical education and their entry into the medical profession in Edinburgh. The author covers a wide range of related issues, various bills and laws, extending the study in medicine by women beyond England to the US, France and India.

Another book in the same field is Edythe Lutzeker's *Medical Education For Women In Great Britain.*[22] This deals with wars waged by Britain in the middle of the nineteenth century and the efforts of pioneers to initiate and carry on a movement for opening medical education to women in Great Britain. The strength of the movement lay in the fact that women patients needed women doctors.

Science in relation to women is a theme in another book, *Hypatia's Heritage*[23] by Margaret Alic. It is a fascinating account of women's contribution to science from prehistory to nineteenth century in Europe. Out of the twelve articles of the collection, three articles relate to women in medicine. Obviously it is valuable on account of devoting some space to a neglected aspect of women's history.

Finally, we may also note a book on women healers of medieval Europe. Authored by Barbara Ehrenreich and Deirdre English, *Witches, Midwives and Nurses A History of Women Healers*[24] has been conceived of as a history of health workers. The book is divided into two phases, one of which is devoted to account of men taking over health care while the other deals with suppression of witches, midwives and nurses in medieval Europe and the rise of male medical profession in the nineteenth century America. Apart from a historical background to health care in medieval Europe, the book also contains numerous photographs and paintings related to the theme.

Another book by the same authors pertains to women and their relation to medical practice and medical beliefs, entitled *Complaints and Disorders: The Sexual Politics of Sickness*[25]. It has been rated quite high by reviewers, as might be clear from a passage cited from it here,

> "The medical system is strategic for women's liberation and oppression. It is the guardian of reproductive technology, birth control, abortion and the means for safe child birth. It holds the promise of freedom from hundreds of unspoken fears and complaints that have handicapped women through out history."[26]

Coming now to the Indian scenario, a pioneering study is that of Charles Leslie even though it does not deal with the Indian Medical Tradition alone, as is reflected in its title *Asian Medical System: A Comparative Study*[27]. It brings out the relation between Asian traditional medicine and modern medicine. The author agrees that all Asian traditional medicines are formulated and rely on a fundamental macro-micro cosmic connection between humans and the world in which they live. All these branches depend on ancient hierarchical textual tradition and all become professional branches of scientific knowledge in Asian countries.

A book that examines the interface of indigenous and western medical system is that of Poonam Bala, *Imperialism and Medicine in Bengal: A Socio-Historical Perspective*[28]. The attitude of British government to indigenous practitioners of medicine in Bengal is taken up for analysis. Essentially a regional study, it highlights the attempt of western system to assert its hegemony over Indian medical practice. She used demographic data concerning medical students of Kolkata. However, she passes over in silence the crucial field of cultural interaction which might have added to her contribution considerably.

The environmental and ideological aspects of the history of health in India have been investigated by Mark Harrison in his remarkable study *Climate and Constitutions: Health, Race, Environment and British Imperialism in India 1600-1850*[29]. It constitutes the first major study of European attitudes towards climate of India and its bearing on in imperial expansion. Utilizing a wide variety source material and extracting evidence from travelogues and original treaties on science and medicine in India, the work contributes substantially to the environmental and medical history of South Asia. It also brings out the nature of oriental discourse with a focus on the racial ideas that went into the shaping of colonial policies. The book reveals that the medical facilities offered by the government were severely disproportionate to the number of natives it was meant for.

Yet another work concerned with medical history on an ideological plane is *Imperial Medicine and Indigenous Societies*[30] edited by David Arnold. Consisting of ten articles, it brings out how western medical knowledge was used as a tool of hegemony by the colonial government. It unfolds the contradictions and rivalries within the imperial order in which medicine and disease acquired importance to formulate and implement official policies. In spite of the valuable contribution it makes to our understanding of relation between ideology and medicine in colonial India, it passes over in silence the field of women's health care. However in another book Arnold does devote some space to the subject, though still largely concerned with the ideological dimension. The review of that book will be in the last section of this paper.

Finally, there is another collection edited by Biswamoy Pati and Mark Harrison. The essays in this anthology, which is entitled *Health, Medicine and Empire: Perspective on Colonial India*,[31] weave together several themes related to the social dimension of the field.

IV

In this last and concluding section we survey a portion of available literature that is partially or wholly devoted to study of women's Health Care which is my special field of interest.

To begin with we will summarise the contents of David Arnold's edited book *Colonizing the Body: State, Medicine, and Epidemic Diseases in Nineteenth Century India.*[32] The major focus of the book is different forms of Indian responses to medical intervention in the context of epidemic diseases. It makes a fascinating story of resistance, accommodation, participation and appropriation. In the process the author highlights the nature and functioning of social dynamics on the Indian scene in terms of internal differentiation and its impact on subaltern politics and middle class hegemony. "Medicine was too powerful, too authoritative a species of discourse and praxis to be left to the colonizers alone."[33] It is noteworthy in the context of this paper that one article deals with women's health care. Captioned "Health and Hegemony", it contains considerable information on women's health conditions, the role of state and the efforts of Christian missionaries towards imparting medical education and training, nature of work done by *dais*, effect of social taboos on Hindu and Muslim women and importing of women doctors in the early stages.

A general history of health is found in Sumit Guha's *Health and Population in South Asia: From Earliest Times to the Present.*[34] Essentially one could classify it as population history in view of its drawing largely on demographic data. In the context of getting better health, the suggestions given include household size, nutrition, sanitation, hygiene, mortality and early propaganda for vaccination. Guha is one of the few historians who has conceded some space to consideration of women's health. The topics of fertility, contraception, mortality and female infanticide find some discussion.

A study exclusively devoted to women's health care was done by Monica Dasgupta and others under the title *Women's Health in India: Risk and Vulnerability.*[35] The authors investigate and document sex differentials with reference to infant and child mortality rates and their relation to socio-cultural and economic factors as also the nature and extent of health risks in the reproductive years. The holistic nature of the study sets it apart as a piece of remarkable research in which women's health from childhood to old age has been covered identifying the points in the life cycle when they are most vulnerable.

Meriting special mention is O. P. Jaggi's volume in the well known series History of Science, Philosophy and Culture in Indian civilization entitled *Medicine In India: Modern Period.*[36] Placing the problem of Indian women of the nineteenth century in correct perspective, he highlights the role of social restrictions and taboos. It is well reflected in the fact,

> "The male doctor if allowed to see a female patient sat behind a screen and felt her pulse. One surgeon was allowed to remove the cataract through a hole cut in a sheet".[37]

Numerous factors contributing to misery of women at the time of child birth, he analyses and notes the instituting of maternal and child welfare schemes at some places in India in the course of the First World War.[38]

Interestingly, we also have a history of health with a nationalist approach. Anil Kumar's *Medicine and the Raj: British Medical Policy in India,* 1835-1911[39] delineates the full scenario of western medicine in colonial India. He attempts to cover the country as a whole, tracing the introduction and growth of medical education, initiation of colonial medical services and official encouragement to medical research in diseases and establishment and growth of hospitals. He also notes the contribution of European women to women's health care and developments in the history of struggle for medical education of women. The role of upper class Indian and European women in raising funds for improvement of Indian women's health care is also highlighted. The collection, interpretation and organization of the data have been done in the form of nationalist critique of colonial government's policies.

Deepak Kumar's *Disease and Medicine in India: A Historical overview*[40] is in origin a collection of papers presented in the course of a panel discussion on the "History of Health conditions and the progress of Medicine in India" held at the 61st session of the Indian History Congress in the year 2000 at Kolkatta. In accordance with the tradition of Indian History Congress, the papers cover all the three periods of Indian history, starting with the life of Harappans and ending with implementation of the health policies of the World Bank. The articles cover a vast area and touch upon a variety of factors, all of which together bring out the richness and plurality of concerns in any history of health and medicine. We have discussions on diseases, health, physicians and codes prescribed for them and medical and surgical practices. As we come to modern India, we have micro-studies of regional problems.

Of special interest for us is the article in the above work, "Disciplining the Body? Health Care for women and children in Early Twentieth Century Bengal"[41] that is devoted to studying the full picture of women's health care in Bengal and the facilities offered by the colonial state in this regard. Activities of the non-official organizations of European women have also been highlighted.

Biswamoy Pati has, however, found serious flaws in the structure and content of the book. In a critical review, we have the categorical assessment, "The non-contributing editor's note, however, shrouds the possibilities the subject holds, is more like ritualized presentation of facts and figures at best or the stumbling block that it remains at worst,.... divides the book into two sections 'premodern' and 'modern'. This is meaningless unless one follows a Euro-centric derivative framework."[42]

Finally the work of Mridula Ramanna, *Western Medicine and Public Health in Colonial Bombay: 1845-1895*,[43] in which clarity of conceptual framework is reflected in the selection of a specific period and the small canvas of a single city to investigate the stages of interface between western medical thinking and the Indian response. The main concern is to locate the impact of western medical ideas and practices on the early institutions of rest and cure in the later half of nineteenth century India. Public health was of primary importance for any regime posing to be benevolent, and in this context colonial paradigms of medical practices and practitioners have to be understood in relation to indigenous ones. To Rammana must be given the credit of being balanced in her evaluation of inconsistencies and errors of judgment for which the entire blame could hardly be laid on the colonial regime. One full chapter has been devoted to discussing medical facilities for women, where we have valuable information on Medical Women India fund, the history of Cama Hospital, women doctors, midwives, nurses and details of problems of women and children. The whole work is based on data from original documents which have been interpreted with critical and analytical approach.

In concluding this rather lengthy survey of historiography on women we can only point out that women's health care must be treated as an area of central concern in the field of women's history or in any project of rewriting women's experiences in mainstream history. Our argument is that, if history is defined as dialogue with the past, then any such dialogue should deal with the subject of fundamental concern in the present, as the experience of the past would give guidelines for the present. For Indian women the subject of fundamental concern is their health which is affected by taboos imposed by traditions and their inbuilt capacity of reproduction which lands them into a variety of health hazards. Women's health does not include their physical well-being alone; it stands for their psychological health as well. It is surprising therefore that women's health care hardly finds any place. The history of women's writing has consistently been occupied with fighting the forces of patriarchy, as is perhaps clear from the survey taken above. What I have done is only a representative survey of historical literature on history of women in India, indicating that it is fairly rich. But this richness in no way contributes to understanding the vast area of women's concern.

References

1. *Toward Equality*, (Government of India, Ministry of Education and Social Welfare, New Delhi, 1974).
2. A.S. Altekar, *The Position of Women in Hindu Civilization* (Delhi, 1959, 2nd edition, Motilal Banarsidass, first published in 1938).
3. Uma Chakravarti, 'Beyond the Altekarian Paradigm: Towards a New Understanding of Gender Relations in Early Indian History' *Social Scientist,* vol. 16, No. 8, 1988, p.48.
4. Ibid, pp.51-2.
5. Gerda Lerner, *The Majority Finds its Past,* (New York, OUP, 1979), p.146.
6. Swami Madhavananda and R.C. Majumdar (eds.), *Great Women of India,* (Almora, Himalayas, Advait Ashram Mayavati, 1953).
7. Padmini Sengupta, *The Story of Women in India* (New Delhi, India Book Company, 1974).
8. S.P. Sen, (ed.), *Dictionary of National Biography* (4 vols. Calcutta, 1972).
9. Tara Ali Baig et. al. (ed.) *Women of India,* (Ministry of Information and Broadcasting, Government of India, 1st edition, 1957, repr. 1990).
10. Indra Gupta, *India's 50 Most Illustrious Women* (New Delhi, Icon Publications Pvt. Ltd., 2003).
11. Gerda Lerner, op. cit. p.166.
12. Ibid, p.146.
13. *Toward Equality* report.
14. Neera Desai, *Women in Modern India,* (Bombay, Vora and Co., 1957).
15. Alfred de Souzas, *Women in Contemporary India: Traditional*

Images and Changing Roles (New Delhi, Manohar Book Service, 1975).

16. Geraldine Forbes *Women in Modern India;* The New Cambridge History of India, IV.2, (New Delhi, Cambridge University Press, 1998).
17. Sushila Nayer and Kamla Mankekar (ed.) *Women Pioneers in India's Renaissance,* (New Delhi, National Book Trust India, 2002).
18. Pratibha Jain and Rajan Mohan, *Women Images* (Rawat Publication, Jaipur, New Delhi, 1996).
19. Kumkum Sangari and Sudesh Vaid (ed.), *Recasting Women: Essays in Colonial History*, (Kali for women, New Delhi, 1989).
20. Kumkum Sangari and Sudesh Vaid (ed.) *Women and Culture* (RCWS, Mumbai, SNDT Women's University, 1994).
21. Sophia Jex-Blake, *Medical Women: A Thesis and A History,* (Edinburgh, Source Book Press, 1986).
22. Edythe Lutzeker, *Medical Education For Women In Great Britain,* (Columbia University, 1959).
23. Margaret Alic, *Hypatia's Heritage: A History of Women in Science from Antiquity to the Late Nineteenth Century* (London, The Women's Press Ltd., 1986).
24. Barbara Ehrenreich and Deirdre English, *Witches, Midwives and Nurses A History of Women Healers* (New York, The Feminist press, 1973).
25. Barbara Ehrenreich and Deirdre English, *Complaints and Disorders: The Sexual Politics of Sickness* (New York, The Feminist Press, 1973).
26. Ibid, p.5.
27. Charles Leslie (ed.), *Asian Medical Systems: A Comparative Study,* Indian Medical Tradition-vol.III, (Delhi, Motilal Banarsidass, 1998).
28. Poonam Bala, *Imperialism and Medicine in Bengal: A Socio-Historical Perspective* (New Delhi, Sage, 1991).
29. Mark Harrison, *Climate and Constitutions: Health, Race, Environment and British Imperialism in India 1600-1850* (New Delhi, OUP, 1999).
30. David Arnold, *Imperial Medicine and Indigenous Societies* (New Delhi, OUP, 1989).
31. Biswamoy Pati and Mark Harrison (ed.) *Health, Medicine and Empire: Perspective on Colonial India*, New Perspective in South Asian History, (Hyderabad, Orient Longman, 2001).
32. David Arnold (ed.) *Colonizing the Body: State, Medicine, and Epidemic Diseases in Nineteenth Century India* (New Delhi, OUP, 1993).

33. Ibid, p.10.
34. Sumit Guha, *Health and Population in South Asia: From Earliest Times to the Present.* (New Delhi, Permanent Black, 2001).
35. Monica Dasgupta et. al. *Women's Health in India: Risk and Vulnerability* (New Delhi, OUP, 1998).
36. O. P. Jaggi, *Medicine In India: Modern Period* in History of Science, Philosophy and Culture in Indian civilization Series (New Delhi, PHISPC, OUP, 2000).
37. Ibid, p.194.
38. Ibid, p.197.
39. Anil Kumar, *Medicine and the Raj: British Medical Policy in India, 1835-1911* (New Delhi, Sage, 1998).
40. Deepak Kumar, *Disease and Medicine in India: A Historical Overview* (New Delhi, IHC, Tulika, 2001).
41. Sujata Mukherjee, 'Disciplining the Body? Health Care for women and children in Early Twentieth Century Bengal' in *Disease and Medicine in India: A Historical Overview* edited by Deepak Kumar, ibid.
42. Economic and Political Weekly, Feb.1, 2003.
43. Mridula Ramanna, *Western Medicine and Public Health in Colonial Bombay: 1845-1895.* New Perspective in South Asian History, (Hyderabad, Orient Longman, 2001).

14

Concepts of Swadeshi and Gender: Tagore's *Ghare Baire*

Sushma J. Varma

Swadeshi is invariably studied in history as a part of the Indian national movement, as the first mass movement in Indian history. This aspect is undoubtedly very important, but it is also necessary to remember that Swadeshi was a concept, and not just a practice. As a concept, it was something that captured the imagination of many people, both at the time of the movement and later. One of the best examples of its impact on the minds of the people of that time can be seen in Rabindranath Tagore's novel, *Ghare Baire*. Its continued hold can be seen in Satyajit Ray's film based on the novel. It tried to show that gender was also one of the issues of the Swadeshi movement, for it was the first time that women were involved in any movement. Tagore's novel brings out this idea, both in the title itself and in the story, for his central character is a woman who moves from just the home to the world outside. In this paper an attempt is being made to focus on the concept of Swadeshi as it emerges in the book and the film, *Ghare Baire*.

Swadeshi emerged as one of the most important theories in 20th century India. The year 1905 is significant in a number of ways. It saw one political action, i.e., the Partition of Bengal, which sparked off a number of responses, politically, socially, intellectually and emotionally.

The novel tries to depict not only a built-in critique of nationalism but also that of the social and cultural realities of the nation. The analysis imposes a psychological sequence on the historical order. It traces the making of the political order by analyzing the political sociology of *Ghare Baire*, through an analysis of the methods of the Swadeshi movement and social reform in general. The focus of both the book and the film is on one upper middle class family, and how they were acting and reacting to Swadeshi. *Ghare Baire*'s literal meaning is 'Home and the World'. As already mentioned, the focal point is women. The experience of Swadeshi is both a reality and a concept, and therefore, it is seen as an experience. The book examines the experience through the five characters, and particularly the women, one of whom experiences it as a silent spectator within the home, while the other steps out of the home, into the world, to experience the movement in the world itself.

Swadeshi has many meanings and facets, some of which are studied in this paper. At one level, Swadeshi was the essence of nationalism. Swadeshi was, at that level, the attachment for and the love of, the country, something which had, by the early years of the 20th century, established a firm hold on the imagination and emotions of the people. However, it was not merely an imaginative exercise, for it was firmly grounded in the economic reality of the time. Swadeshi was therefore an economic concept, which promoted the idea of the use of indigenous goods. At the time, it was, therefore, one of the major theories defining and defending economic nationalism. Through this economic base, and the feelings of patriotism, Swadeshi therefore promoted self-sufficiency, self-respect, and self-reliance.

Swadeshi was, in other words, from the beginning, both theory and practice. Patriotism was linked to power, the power of *Atmasakti* or the mother. As practice, as it was rooted in both emotion and practicality, it was both constructive and destructive. These aspects continue to inform the concept of Swadeshi even today. Swadeshi continues to mean different things to different people. For politicians, it is an ideology.

For the common man, it is the use of Indian goods, and so, it means self-respect. But the economists and industrialists were aware of the limitations of Swadeshi even at the height of the movement. All these aspects can be seen both in the book and in the film.

Characters of the Story

The story revolves around three main characters, two male and one female and two subordinate characters, one male and one female. Each understood Swadeshi in his or her own terms, and an attempt is being made to show how each one of them propagated Swadeshi, as they understood it.

The first character is Nikhil, a rich and popular landlord. He was educated in the liberal tradition and was an enlightened intellectual, who understood the theory and practice of Swadeshi. He extended his liberalism to his wife Bimala, the second character, but the one around whom the entire story revolves, whom he educated. He wanted her to leave her traditional seclusion and enter the larger world and then make her own rational choices. She was caught between the theory and practice of Swadeshi movement. The third character, Sandip was a leader of the Swadeshi movement. He perhaps represents Tagore's own uneasiness with the nature of the leadership of the time, for Sandip is portrayed as one who is self-motivated, and accepting the ideology of Swadeshi only because he sees benefit in it for himself.

The subordinate characters are, first of all, Amulya. A student and an emotional follower of the movement, he is shown to be growing more aware of the reality in the process of the book, and therefore, the character represents both, the gap between theory and practice, and the growing awareness, in public consciousness, of that gap. The female character is Nikhil's sister-in-law, an uneducated young widow, who remained within the home, but by observation alone, could make a critical analysis of the Swadeshi movement, and could therefore understand that Swadeshi was both constructive and destructive. She is portrayed as being witness to the destruction of her world, which offers security and continuity, by the entry of the outside world into that closed environment. She therefore is the representation of the title again, but in a slightly modified form, for in her case, it is not the home *and* the world, but the home *vs.* the world.

Story

The story begins with the death of Nikhil's elder brother. He had great sympathy for his widowed sister-in-law, who though financially secure did not know how to pass the time in doing something constructive. So when he got married he decided that he would educate his wife Bimala. He appointed a Governess to teach her not only English, but also etiquette, style, dress etc. Nikhil is shown as being perfectly in tune with the middle and upper classes of the time, who promoted the cause of women's education, but only partly because of their own belief in its value. The women were to be educated not for their own sake, but because they were to show the 'enlightened' outlook of their husbands. They were, in a sense, showpieces, who were thus on public display. As the public display necessarily involved the colonial masters, these women had to 'fit' into the society of the time. Bimala came up to the expectations of her husband, for she learnt all that was expected of her. The novel also shows one aspect of the awakening of nationalism in India. Just as nationalism was sparked off by exposure to western ideologies and theories, which then resulted in questioning of the forms of colonialism, so also, Bimala is shown to be increasing her powers of perception through questioning the world around her.

The next character to be introduced is Nikhil's friend Sandip, who had become a leader of the Swadeshi movement. Friends from college days, Nikhil had initially envied Sandip's ability to attract people. Sandip is shown to be an extrovert, quick to impress people, but basically self-serving, in contrast to Nikhil, who was a strong, rational and pragmatic person. Nikhil was not part of the movement, but was a person who took his responsibilities seriously. He is portrayed as a person with integrity, whose conscience ruled his mind, while with Sandip it was the reverse. Nikhil was keen on introducing

Sandip to his wife. Bimala was initially reluctant. But since he was determined, she agreed[1]. However, when she met him she was highly impressed. Nikhil on the other side was proud to introduce his wife to his friend. Subconsciously he may even have wanted him to be attracted to her.

Bimala was highly impressed by Sandip's speeches on Swadeshi. She discussed them with her husband, who, however, was rather doubtful about the real validity of Swadeshi. He is portrayed as believing that Sandip's nationalism was only another form of covetousness. A practical man, he analysed Swadeshi in terms of its value to the people of his village. He believed that Swadeshi was impractical, for it would be hard on the poor traders who would be forced to sell indigenous goods of inferior quality at higher cost. Swadeshi would result in greater problems, for the peasants did not have the money to buy these goods. He believed that survival came before nationalism, for if there was only poverty, then the nation could not even be created, let alone consolidated. This was a rational enlightened way of looking at the problem. At the same time Nikhil was fully aware of the political situation of the time, and knew that he could not stay out of the activities of the period entirely, no matter what his reservations. As he also felt that one should work for one's own people, he started a soap factory, an oil crusher mill and whatever else was within his scope and power to promote small business in his estate. Realizing the financial problems faced by most people in his village, he also tried to find banks to give loans to people. Unconsciously he was propagating Swadeshi, in his own way. This was a real and constructive Swadeshi.

At the same time, the destructive element in Swadeshi is also brought out. The soap factory had been handed over to a businessman, and the soap was both sold in the village shops and brought to the house. Nikhil's sister-in-law is here shown to bring out the destructive element, for she criticized the soap that was made, declaring that it was not even fit for cleaning vessels with. Her comments made Nikhil aware of the problems arising out of desire for profit, which took precedence over the requirements of the people. Though the businessman does not actually appear in either the book or the film, yet he is shown to be, at the micro-level, a variation of the selfishness that characterized Sandip, and perhaps Swadeshi itself.

Therefore those who understood it felt it was their duty to create awareness among the people. Some were committed to it sincerely, while some just for the sake of popularity were able to influence the people with their charismatic personality. Sandip was able to do this. He preached Swadeshi and could influence many youngsters. Some even dropped out of school to help him. Amulya was one such student who wholeheartedly supported Sandip and did many things for him. This is what one can call emotional Swadeshi. To promote Swadeshi one needed manpower plus finance.

For financial aid, Sandip looked to Bimala. Both the book and the film trace the increasing hold that Sandip was acquiring on Bimala. This again can be seen as emotional Swadeshi, for though Bimala was, at some level, aware of the basic selfishness of Sandip, she nevertheless was carried away by a sense of attachment, to the nation through Sandip. Nikhil realised what was going on, but did not prevent her either from giving him money or meeting him. He was willing to risk his marriage, so that his wife could have strength and freedom. He therefore represents Tagore's ideas of the new nation that was to come-aware, strong, rational, and above all, free to choose the correct path.

Sandip had none of these qualities. He appears to be merely play acting as a leader of the movement. The role of leader gives him the public image that he needs, while that of wooer of Bimala gives him a place in a home. Here again, the binary of the home and the world is brought out. Sandip is portrayed as needing Bimala for his pleasure and finance, i.e., for his own world, and the larger world outside him. However, here, as the character of Sandip is shown to be selfish, both his worlds are only reflections of different aspects of his own character. Bimala is shown as representing, in one female body, all that he desires. He needs to see her every day, there is a sense of desperation behind his joking references to Bimala as "Queen Bee". He could not afford to make this explicit to Bimala, for then she too would be alienated from him, and so, he explains such references in terms of the mother cult, atma shakti, which was an important part of the Swadeshi movement. Sandip was least interested in the Swadeshi ideology, which, for him, was only a means of self-glorification. In this, he was not alone, for there were others who were willing to subvert the ideology of Swadeshi for their own ends. Sandip was in alliance with an old estate manager who agreed to sink a boat bringing in British goods and later on he threatened to burn the crops of the peasants if they did not join the movement. This was Swadeshi as power. Sandip realised the potential of Swadeshi for self-aggrandisement, through its use as a tool of coercion. One of the earliest characters to understand him was Amulya. The student, who had left his studies in response to the charisma of Sandip, began to realise that the movement, as represented by Sandip, was in no sense a 'national' one. He tried to make Bimala aware of what exactly Sandip was doing, saying, among other things, that a good part of her donation was going to support Sandip's high living and then jokingly saying that a simple style of living damaged a leader's strength. Amulya was able to make Bimala more aware, and she started examining Sandip critically. Her perception of the world changed in accordance with her involvement in it. She began to understand that Sandip was mainly a talker, a persuader, that he craved power and would do anything to get it, including causing bloodshed between the Hindus and Muslims. His form of Swadeshi was for power, or rather, the exploitation of Swadeshi for personal benefit. Both Bimala and Amulya realised that they were caught and that now it was too late and difficult to come out of it.

Increasingly, Bimala became aware of the difference between the practices of Nikhil and Sandip. The former understood the reality of colonialism, and realised that Swadeshi was a means of attacking colonialism, but it required greater understanding, and greater application at the grassroots level. He was, in other words, aware of the world, its reality, and wanted to work to change it. However, he knew that change had to be initiated at a very basic level, and so he began with his own estate. In some ways, he represents the coming together of the home and the world, for to him, the world of action was the familiar, the 'home' of the estate. Sandip, on the other hand, saw in Swadeshi nothing but a means of acquiring more power. He was unconcerned with the realities of colonialism and Swadeshi was the world, for to him, the people were merely tools to be used to his own advantage.

At the end of the book, communal riots break out, as a result of Sandip's propaganda. Nikhil goes out in an attempt to control the riot, but is killed. Bimala, as a widow, then decides to continue the work of her husband, on the estate. She is thus shown as stepping out of the home, into the world, but the world of the estate and her dead husband.

Ghare Baire is thus a story rooted in a historical time and space. The dichotomy between the two, the attempts to negotiate the two, and the final resolution, of this dichotomy, is shown in the way in which the character of Bimala is developed. It is significant that the main protagonist is a woman, for this was the first time in India's history that women became part of a movement outside the home. This, historically, was also the time of the spread of the idea of "Mother India", something that acquired much greater force later. The novel therefore represents the idea of strength as woman. While not a feminist text, it is nevertheless one that places a woman at the centre of events. It thus marks the development of a certain mentality, associated with that phase of nationalism, of the woman as having a role to play, and therefore as being part of the nation. Thus, both the book and the film mark the emergence of woman as having a distinct identity, linked with both, the home and the world, or from the home to the world.

References

1. Ashis Nandy, *The Illegitimacy of Nationalism*, OIP 1994, p. 13, points out that Bimala's first instincts about Sandip were that

he was a professional politician and therefore inauthentic. She is nevertheless attracted to him.

2. This paper is an attempt to theorise Swadeshi on the basis of a novel, written at the time of the movement. It is therefore difficult to follow orthodox research methodology in the form of detailed footnoting and an extensive bibliography. Other than the book itself, the following works have been used:

   Nandy, Ashis, *The Illegitimacy of Nationalism*, OIP, Delhi, 1994

   Tagore, S.N. (tr.), *The Home and the World*, Macmillan, Madras, 1919.

   Ghare-Baire – a photocopied article in the library of the National Film Archives, Pune, unknown author, unknown journal, pp. 188-199.

15

Gender Relations in Indian National Army

Manisha Dikholkar

During World War II, Indians abroad in South East Asia and East Asia were politically roused and united in one organization. In East Asia over two million Indians were organized and inspired by the slogan of 'Total Mobilization' of the Army of Liberation i.e. the *Azad Hind Fauj* organized by the Indian Independence League in East Asia. The League set up the Provisional Government of Azad Hind and conducted the last fight for Indian freedom with the help of Azad Hind Fauj.

The Indian National Army was formed on September 1, 1942. Captain Mohan Singh was appointed as Commander. Recruitment was done from the Indian soldiers who had surrendered in Malaya and nearly 7000 well-disciplined troops were raised. The Indian National Army Act that was specially prepared in August 1942 governed the army.

The idea organizing the Indians for self-defense and to fight for India's Independence received encouraging but cautious support.Netaji Subhash Chandra Bose arrived in Singapore on July 2, 1943. On 4th July a conference of delegates from all countries in East Asia assembled. Rash Behari Bose formally handed over presidentship of the India Independence League to Subhash Chandra Bose. On the same day Netaji addressed a meeting of Indian delegates, he sounded the call of 'Total Mobilization' of men and material in East Asia to wage war against Britain. Total Mobilization included four things 1) Men 2) Money, 3) Sources and 4) Unity. He further made it clear that 'men' meant women and children as well. He said that women had to play an important part in the glorious struggle that lay before them. Women must share the responsibilities of their men folk, lighten the burden of their work, and finally if need be fight, suffer and die on the battlefield. On that very occasion men and women offered money and jewelry to Netaji for the sake of the motherland. On an earlier occasion in 1928, Bose in his address at the Maharashtra Provincial Conference had pronounced, "It is impossible for one half of the nation to win liberty without the active sympathy and support of the other half".[1]

In a meeting held on July 9, 1943 he desired all members of the society to get involved in the work. In the same meeting he suggested opening a Women's Regiment, which would be named the Rani Jhansi Regiment.

Laxmi Swaminathan, an Indian medical practitioner in Singapore, was connected with the Indian Independence League and helped the League in its medical relief work and occasionally she used to give talks on radio. On July 14, 1943, Laxmi was appointed secretary of Women's department of the Indian Independence League Headquarters. She believed that it was the duty of every Indian in the Far East to train himself or herself in the use of modern methods of warfare and to fight and defeat Britain and free our motherland. She herself wanted to join the military services suggested by Netaji.

In the beginning stiff opposition came from some men against the very idea of women being enrolled as combatants. They maintained that women should be enlisted as nurses and that actual fighting with arms should be left to men alone.

But in spite of opposition Netaji remained firm in his decision that women should, if needed, fight shoulder to shoulder with men. In the Far East women themselves were ready to welcome any opportunity to take up arms and fight on the battlefield. By this they could kill two birds with one stone. One, they could serve the motherland by participating in Indian National Army and secondly, they could come out of the home and emancipate themselves from the patriarchal society of the time. Women could become equal to men.

Barrister Yellapa and Laxmi had organized one special meeting of Netaji to address only women. For this meeting to give salutation they trained 20 young women. On this occasion 20 young women including Laxmi gave honour of salutation to Netaji with rifles in their hands. He was very much impressed by this act on the part of women.

From 14th July, Laxmi had started work as Commander of the Regiment and organizer of the women's wing. Initially 100 women joined the training and camp. In the meantime Laxmi went on a tour of Penang Ipoha, Kuala Lumpur and Selongore and recruited a large number of women. One such woman named Smt. Satyawati Thiwar who was the Principal of a school came to Singapore with Laxmi and became an expert in warfare activities. They had to work in a very systematic and disciplined manner. Being a woman, there was no excuse for women.

In October 1943, Netaji officially inaugurated the 'Rani Jhansi Regiment'. Initially 150 women joined the army, and their number soon went up to 300. In the same month, Netaji also formed Arz-i-Hukumat-Azad-i-Hind, i.e. Provisional Government of Free India. At the same time Laxmi was appointed as a Cabinet Minister for the Welfare of Women and Children in the Provisional Government of Free India. She was already a chairperson of the Women's Wing of Indian Independence League. Laxmi started her double duty as Minister and that of providing military and nursing training to women for the army. Laxmi was given a Commission and was straightway honored with a rank of a Captain.

It was decided to send trained officers, women soldiers and nurses of Rani Jhansi Regiment to Rangoon. After completing training there, they were to be sent on the battlefield for actual fighting against the enemy. When Laxmi went to Bangkok, Netaji himself and many other officers welcomed her and the Government of Thailand honored her as a Cabinet Minister. Indeed it was great honor not only to Laxmi but also to Indian Womanhood. She was given the honour, opportunities, duties and responsibilities as given to any other male Cabinet Minister.

In the army women also had exercise training, rifle training and day and night walking route march like their male counterparts. In addition they had to take nursing training. They were getting training to live a hard life. Before joining all women were given the idea that they would have to live a hard life, and they should be ready to die for the motherland. Psychologically all women were prepared for such hardships.

On March 30, 1944, eight young women became Commissioned Officers. They had to pass all written and oral examinations as well as demonstrate warfare and military skills successfully, like male Commissioned Officers. Women started their training before sunrise and ended after sunset. It is a noteworthy fact that women who once joined the military services never gave it up. On the contrary everyday there were new recruitments. Women were given pistols and rifles. As the Lee Enfield 303 rifle was too heavy for women to handle, they were given rifles made on Dutch model that were easier to handle. Now in every respect women were ready to go to the front for actual fighting along with men.

All the women in the Regiment were known as 'Rani'. Most of the women were labourers from the Rubber Plantation in Malaya, and not literate. Educated women received officers' training. Women from different communities such as Hindu, Muslim and Christian joined the army and there was no discrimination on the ground of religion or caste. All lived together, ate together, worked together and learned the art of guns and machineguns, rifles. They had to walk almost 30 miles everyday and then spend 1-2 hours nursing the wounded soldiers. Women from all ages such as 13-year-old Maya Ganguly up to 40-year-old Satyawati Thiwar all joined military camp. Later their number increased and went up to 1500.

It is noteworthy that girls below 13 and women above 40 were also desirous to join the army. But as a rule they were not allowed in the army. To satisfy elderly women Netaji allowed them to cook for the soldiers and accompany them on their way to battlefield.

Bal-Sena

For boys and girls below 13, Netaji started Bal-Sena. With the view of instilling in them love for their motherland, faith, service and unity were taught to them. In every city of Burma and Malaya they started one division of Bal-Sena. They were trained for three weeks in the camp. The first camp was started near Rangoon. Children were trained on the model of military training, which included rifle training. In spite of the hard work all children enjoyed their training. Not only that, some of them were also sent to enemy's camp to put bombshells. It was like a suicide squad and was very daring on their part.

The activities of Bal-Sena included taking out processions with the tricolor flag in hands, to shout slogans such as 'Netaji Zindabad' and 'Azad Hind Fauj Zindabad'. When British conquered Mandalay, they put a ban on the slogan 'Jai-Hind'. But these children from Bal-Sena used to shout slogans wherever they saw the British police and used to act bravely and fearlessly. The British Police got tired of them.

After three weeks of training these girls and boys used to train children from their area. Besides this, their duty included helping the needy, collecting money for Netaji and Indian National Army along with propaganda work. A batch comprising of 40 children of 15 years old were sent to Tokyo for Navy, air and military training. They were called Tokyo Cadets.

Men and women offered their money and jewelry for the cause of Azad Hind Fauj. They were given a title like Sewak-i-Hind and Sevika-i-Hind. One such woman named Hiraben Betai from Rangoon (originally from Saurashtra) had given diamonds and jewelry worth five lakhs. Men like Nizazi, Basir

Ahmed gave money and received Sewak-i-Hind title from Netaji and Azad Hind Fauj.

Social Background

The Indian women in Singapore and East Asia belonged to either the middle or the lower classes. They were not very well aware of equality and freedom, as their families were orthodox. Their main interest was their home and family. Under such circumstances it is noteworthy that large numbers of women responded to the call of Netaji and later became prisoners of war.

The Indian National Army provided men and women an opportunity to participate in the public sphere through movement. Women did not reject their domestic role but used it as a base to give them strength and legitimacy in their demands. Their activities have created a deep awareness about the freedom movement. It illustrates how women's activities negotiate certain situations to transcend the boundaries prescribed for them.

Women's participation in Indian National Army saw redefinitions of their roles from domestic guardians of the private sphere into equal participants as individuals or the citizens of the state.

References

1. S.C. Bose, *Collected Works,* Volume I, Oxford University Press, 1985, p. 149.
2. Ayer, S. A. *The Indian Independence Movement in East Asia* (Netaji, Nation, 1961) Bulletin of the Netaji Research Bureau, Calcutta, 1961.
3. Bala, Usha and Sharma, Anshu, *Indian Women Freedom Fighters 1857-1947,* Manohar Publication, New Delhi, 1986.
4. Bharava, M. L., *Netaji Subhash Chandra Bose in South East Asia and India's Liberation War 1943-45,* Vishwavidhya Publishers, Malayattor, 1982.
5. Bose, S. C. Netaji, *Collected works*, Volume I, Oxford University Press, New Delhi, 1985.
6. Chander, Jagpravesh, *Meet Colonel Laxmi,* India Private Works, Karachi Road, Lahore, 1946.

7. Chopra, P. N. *Women in the Freedom Struggle,* Ministry of Education and Social Welfare, New Delhi, 1975.
8. Gosh, K. K. *Indian National Army: Second Front of the Independence Movement*, Meenakshi, Meerut, 1969.
9. Garware R. *Captain Laxmi and Rani Jhansi regiment*, Sadhana Prakashan, Pune 1998 (Verse Marathi)
10. Jhaveri, V. K. (Ed.) *Jaihind – The Story of a Rebel Daughter of India with the Rani of Jhansi Regiment,* Janmbhoomi Prakashan Mandir, Bombay, 1945.

16

Freedom Movement in Assam: A Perspective on Gender Inequality

Ranjana Mishra

Introduction

Gender discrimination was an obvious phenomenon in India before independence. A male child was always preferred to a female one, boys were privy to getting higher education while girls were assigned the job of helping mother in the household. Girls were married off early and young. It was a taboo for a lady to go to public life. Yet there were notable figures like Rani Laxmibai and Kasturba Gandhi. Fortunate were those who were inspired by their parents for patriotic jobs and encouraged by husbands to continue their patriotism. A galaxy of Assamese women turned out to be such patriots in the freedom struggle of India. However, history has not treated them kindly. A fair deal to fair sex has remained a daydream. Harking back to the annals of patriarchal society, one discovers a vast array of endocentric activities, where voices of women are largely ignored. The role of gender, particularly that of women within the household, the division of labour in the productive sphere of activities, and in other political and cultural arenas often reinforces two aspects:

(i) Women are made to confine themselves to the household and remain busy in child bearing, offspring rearing and nursing. The maximum they could stretch is into the realm of music, dance and literature; thus uplifting the cultural level of the family and the society at large. Work outside the confines of house was well nigh impossible. From the margins of society to the mainstream of national liberation movement, it was a momentous journey for most women. The picture was dizzier in the Northeast than elsewhere.

(ii) Women's role in the realm of politics and economy is normally perceived through the prism of men, who act as assessor and appraiser of the role played by women. This asymmetric, gender based perception has been defined through the heroic deeds of few valorous women, whose contribution to the freedom struggle of India remains indelible. At the grass root level, aflame with enthusiasm sparked by leaders like Mahatma Gandhi, these women threw their fate into the mainstream of public awakening. Cutting across caste-creed barriers of a largely rural India, they came out from mediaeval bondage with courage to throw out the British rulers from their native Indian soil. It is the history of these women that tells us sagacious details of our freedom struggle.

The role of these women at the micro level has not been adequately studied. Although some efforts at assessing the feminine role have been made at macro level, a lot remains to be done, particularly when it comes to undertaking in-depth study of women freedom fighters at the provincial level and down below. Based on consecutive three years of case studies and personal interviews with Assamese woman freedom fighters,[1] this paper makes a micro attempt to highlight the role of few women of Assam - then a unified territory out of which half a dozen states have been carved out in independent India. Bordering with one of the pioneering states of the Indian national liberation movement, undivided Bengal and motivated by the inherent inclination of patriotism, these women had fought for their empowerment, gender equality and human rights in patriarchal set up to free it from the shackles of age-old bondage.

Literature Review

The existing literature on role of women in the freedom struggle in Northeast India throws little light on details of local incidents. However, a few of them such as Anita Mishra's article entitled "Gender Sensitization of Grassroot" brought out in 1998, argues that women have not only been a victim of the age old social and cultural limitations; but also of the "discriminatory competitive market forces".[2] Bibekanand Das and L.N. Das in the book "The Feminine Gender"[3] write that taking a worldwide view one can, without controversy, accept the proposition that women enjoy a lower status compared to men. In order to bridge this gap, gender equality ought to be ensured and more rights should be given to women. For instance, women's economic and political rights, their social development, mitigation and elimination of gender-based discrepancies should forthwith be done away with.

The core of the problem lay in the low literacy level of women vis-à-vis men in British India in general and remote regions like Assam in particular. With only one University set up in 1857 in Kolkata by the British, it is logically presumed that higher education was a domain inaccessible to most women. If at all they studied, they completed matriculation and then devoted themselves to the household. Thus we have a two-fold picture in hand; some of the women, albeit with less qualifications, were married only to the cause of national liberation 'they did not marry at all to raise a family'; others, who married and raised a family, became freedom fighters under the shadow of their politically influential husbands.

From a feminine perspective, the patriarchal set-up compels women to subordination, subservience and dependence on men. It locks her in daughter-wife-mother triangle without providing her access to any socially acceptable alternatives as an independent individual and treats her primarily as an instrument of male sexual enjoyment by assigning her the task of perpetuating his species. As a result, women have little control over economic resources and are reduced not only to economic dependence, but also to resultant social and legal deprivations of status in a male dominated world without any property rights.[4]

In the midst of the entire scholastic generalisation, what sets Assam apart is the uniqueness of the position of woman in the Assamese society. Evidences from the Gazetteer of Assam and "History of Assam" by Edward Gait suggest that in comparative terms, Assamese women were socially better off than women in other parts of India. For example, a young woman in the Garo society had the privilege of choosing her own husband. The children took the clan name of the mother instead of the father, as this was a matriarchal rather than a patriarchal society. However, consensual divorce was allowed on the grounds of infidelity, adultery and barrenness. Thus, despite living free from what is known as a rigid patriarchy, one could find Assamese women to be victims of gender discrimination. Rural women from past through present continue to be the backbone of Assam's subsistence agricultural economy. Tea plantation workers, mostly women, live in constant inequality. In a research conducted by Guwahati University's Centre for economic development and administration in 1998, on the "status of women in Assam", it was estimated that on average women worked 10.81 hours each day compared to 7.51 hours put in by men. Women did 88 per cent of all domestic activities, 69 per cent of village work and 63 per cent of agricultural activities. However, of all the earnings outside the home, men earned 69 per cent. Men take most of the decisions on how the money is to be spent. Property transactions, sale of animals or major household loans primarily remain a man's prerogative. Thus, outside earning capacity along with access to the market places put men into the job of bargaining and selling and consequently in an advantageous position. They gained confidence in decision making while women were relegated to the household to take care of the family.[5]

While this has been the condition of rural women folk, in retrospect, we see that women of Assam have rendered yeomen' service to their state in the political, social and economic spheres. Why then in the country's freedom movement, have their names remained obscure? The answer to this question lies in the endemic gender inequality prevalent in the Assamese society. While their male counterparts have been mentioned in all the Government Gazetteers and have a place in all the books written on the freedom struggle, most of the literature purposely ignored women freedom fighters. Thus literature on the freedom movement remains largely endocentric although a few important names of women freedom fighters have appeared off and on, here and there.

A recent book by Dipti Sharma and Anuradha Dutta[6] had highlighted the role of women in the freedom struggle movement. However, their painstaking study does not include women freedom fighters from lower Assam valley, thus ignoring a large segment of participants. Assam was one of the last victims of British imperialism in India, losing her independence after the signing of the Treaty of Yandabo in 1826. Yet Assam was one of the earliest to rise in revolt against the shackles of foreign rule, when it joined the mainstream of the country's struggle for freedom. Far too long have Assamese women been accustomed to value the freedom of their motherland better than their lives. The glorious tradition of Ramani Gabharu and Mula Gabharu, who had taken up arms to safeguard the honour of the throne, had continued to inspire Assamese women. That tradition was further enriched by the heroic sacrifices of young women such as Rangili and Padumi. However, when the dream of Assamese women for a united and free India did not materialize even after innumerable sacrifices, they had to wait until the advent of a man like Mahatma Gandhi whose magic call had aroused an entire nation to awake the country from a deep slumber.

Sharma and Dutta further elucidated that from 1915 onwards, the women of Assam began to organize themselves. The women of Dibrugarh were the first to organize a Samiti of their own. By 1926 their organizational network had spread to the provincial level. They contributed significantly to the freedom movement either individually or through their local associations. In all the three major national movements in 1921, 1930 and 1942, quite a few women like Nalinibala Devi, Malati Phookan, Sumita Bhattacharya, Smita Barua, Chandraprova Saikiani, Shrijuta Rajbala Das, Suvarnalata Barua, Rohini Gohain, Basantlata Hazarika, Sarhi Prabha Hazarika, Muktabala Baishnavi, Mohini Gohain, Dariki Kachari, Mangri, Smt. Swaranlata Barua, Amol Prova Das, Kanaklata Phuleshwari Devi, Bhogeswari Phukanani and many others had participated. These women had contributed through various acts like picketing in front of wine and opium shops, forming barricades in front of government institutions, setting up squads they struck fear into the hearts of the British imperialist rulers. Despite warnings, threats, fines, lathi charges, firing, short or longer terms of imprisonment etc. their spirit of revolt did not die down; instead their participation increased.

Most telling was the sterling fervour of patriotism among rural women. There were many illiterate or semi-literate women from rural areas imprisoned during the freedom struggle movement. Their role was either totally neglected or ignored. Corroborating these neglected aspects by taking up a few case studies of still living women freedom fighters, who participated actively during 1940's in individual *satyagraha* and Quit India movement, an attempt is made here to throw light on some of the least known feminine figures of our freedom struggle. Although a patriarchal set-up has put their names on the backburner of obscurity, they remain the source of oral history in Assam's districts. They are living embodiment of the movement that fetched us freedom.

Case Studies

Swarnalata Mohanto[7], a social worker turned freedom fighter in the district of Sonitpur was born in 1924. She joined the civil disobedience movement at the tender age of seven along with her mother and maternal uncle. She took active part in the singing squad to collect funds for the Congress party. She learnt spinning and wove khadi caps from hand-spun yarn for freedom fighters. Between 1937-41 she managed single-handedly and did the work for Parbatia Swadeshi Mahila Samiti. Suspended from her school for a month and deprived of her scholarship for protesting against the orders of anti-national government along with another freedom fighter, Nirmala Das at Barbakari, Swarnalata was defiant despite all her vicissitudes. In 1942, she pledged not to marry. Her marriage was scheduled for August 1942, a time when Quit India movement had begun. Keeping in tune with the true devotion of a nationalist to a cause more sublime than marital bliss, Swarnalata preferred the life of freedom fighter to that of a housewife.

In 1942, upon directions from the Congress, the Sootea Congress Mahila Sabha opened a total of 62 branches across Sonitpur district. She organised various strikes, processions, and meetings and formed the women's nursing squad and later the death squad. She hoisted the national flag atop the Sootea police station for which she underwent imprisonment along with three of her women compatriots of Sootea Mahila Sabha. Subsequently, she was directed to work underground. She did this job with missionary zeal. Along with Pramila Barua, she met late Gahan Goswami, the then in charge of the underground section of the District Congress Committee and discussed with him the roadmap for future activities. Against tight governmental security, she was able to pass on the "documents" and papers of revolutionary activities to late Padma Bhushan, Bijay Bhagwati's sister without being caught and flawlessly fled underground amidst neck-high paddy fields and jungles. Finally, she was arrested and put into Tezpur jail for three months.

In 1947, she attended the meeting of Gandhiji at Guwahati. Inspired by his exhortations, she spearheaded the women Seva Dal to organised talks on untouchability across the districts of lower Assam. This enabled her to persuade the untouchables to enter the Hajo temple in 1948, thus demolishing a taboo that Harijans are forbidden to enter the temple. She had a brief stint at Wardha between 1949-50. She got the offer for the post of headmistress from a Guwahati school, but on the advice of late Bijay Bhagwati; she declined that offer, and instead, took up a job of schoolteacher at Sootea. Her selfless devotion to the society continued uninterrupted through teaching and social upliftment of the downtrodden.

Well into the sixties, the revolutionary spirit still continued to enthuse her. During 1962 Chinese aggression, she organised villagers and gave them military training. Besides, she collected gold and clothes from the villagers and sent them to government as financial and material help to the soldiers and their families. She opened six branches of the Mahila Samiti that ran regular activities like weaving, spinning, knitting and sericulture. She also set up *Balwadi* and study circles. The *Balwadi* at North Sootea and the sericulture farm at east Sootea are embodiment of her institutions still functioning.

With the burning desire to serve the nation, she contested the election, won it with a thumping majority and became a Minister of State in 1972. Unfortunately, she had to resign on 8th February 1976 to make way for a male aspirant. Politics took its ugly turn on a women freedom fighter. A revolutionary woman of her calibre, who opened 14 sericulture farms, introduced *Tassar* weaving in North Cachar Hills and opened General Peoples cooperatives remained untold and unsung.

Poor health had made Swarnalata Mohanto weak. Living in a dilapidated home sans luxury without any means of constructing a modern house and refusing to go in for medical treatment, her condition remained pathetic. Despite her intense desire to be a part of present day politics, her male counterparts effectively sidetracked her from active politics. This struggle of a solitary woman freedom fighter speaks eloquently of the existing gender inequality at the micro level politics in our country.

Another woman of valour, whose contribution to Assam's freedom struggle was immense, was Pushpalata Das[8]. Born on 27 March 1915 at Lakhimpur, tempered herself in the arduous journey to freedom. At the age of six she distributed leaflets, containing Gandhiji's message. She joined "Banar Sena" to popularise Khadi among the people and organised

"Charkha Sangh". Even her father, a government employee, was compelled by his little daughter to wear only Khadi. Inspired by her mother; she took the pledge for freedom and never looked back. By coming into contact with several frontline leaders of the freedom movement, she converted herself to a pure Gandhian. She was selected by Gandhiji for individual *Satyagraha* and remained in jail for two and half months as an under-trial. She was suspended from school for taking part in individual *Satyagraha*. During Quit India movement, she was arrested and jailed for 3 years. Due to illness, the government was forced to release her on parole. However, her refusal to be released earned her accolades from Gandhiji. She had organised Mrittu Vahini (death squads) in which 15 martyrs faced bullets and Assam's heroic Kanaklata was one of them.

She was a member of the Rajya Sabha between 1950 and 1960 and significantly contributed to the debates in the house. At the time of voting, she once opposed Jawaharlal Nehru's resolution of the working committee; and that was an apparent signal of her political death. She continued to be the president of Kasturba Memorial Trust. Involved in many social activities, a tireless fighter for social justice, she had been partially successful in putting an end to the Northeast insurgencies by persuading quite a few terrorists to surrender. When offered "Tamra Patra" by the Government, she refused to accept and wrote to the then chief minister of Assam Shri Sarat Chandra Sinha: "with all my profound sense of gratitude to the well wishes of the Government, I would like to say humbly that I did not take part in the freedom movement with an intention to get anything in return. That was complete by itself with joy, so I could not like to accept your honour...Let the beauty of service remain animated". These words, perhaps, rightly reflect her feelings and thoughts of sacrifice. She had donated her entire Padma Bhushan award money for betterment of the downtrodden. Living in a small two-room house in the twilight zone of life, a valiant soldier remained extraordinarily optimistic. An in-depth analysis of her views reveal that half of the insurgencies in the Northeast could have been resolved by persuasion, if these humble women visionaries were given a say in the present political scenario. What restrains them from doing their duty for the nation is the domination of male over women in the given political scenario.

Similarly, Pramila Barua's contribution to the Assamese freedom struggle may appear modest, but the spirit and devotion behind it makes it all the more significant and memorable. Born on 15 December 1928 in Tezpur, she jumped into the freedom struggle in 1942. Like many others, the Quit India events of 1942 had sparked anti-British ideas in the mind of Barua. She gathered 100 volunteers during individual *Satyagraha* form a Mahila Sevika Dal to work at night to disseminate secret news to underground freedom fighters. This group used to organise rallies, where inspiring patriotic couplets were sung of which just one is reproduced below:

> *Vishwa Vijayi Nawjawan Taikariba Lagiba Agnisaman Ulkpath Bajrapat, Hoshiyar, Hoshiyar*[9] World conqueror youth, be like fire, lightning and thunder, remain alert. Hoshiyar[9]

In 1942, during the Quit India movement, she was arrested but overcrowding of the jail facilitated her release. She was an active member of the Tezpur Mahila Samiti, which was established in 1928 in Assam. In 1947, the Tezpur Mahila Samiti extended its organisational activities by federating a large number of primary, village Mahila Samitis into it. Barua was, however, never offered a rank in politics. After independence, she took up the job of a teacher and continued her social work. She motivated women to join cooperative societies and persuaded them to be self-reliant. Till a short while ago, she kept organising plays to infuse confidence in women. Many of her plays were staged in Assam. Some of her famous popular plays are Karangar, Ligari, Bandini, Kalyani, Jay Mati and Dhatte Panna. She was not happy with the present day circumstances in Assam and in the country. Education, awareness and economic independence are these crucial aspects of Barua's thought for women. The social malaise and political corruption that cripple Assam these days perturbs her. However, this optimistic lady has great hopes that she pins on the teachers to mould the young generation in such a way that they would feel proud of their nation and devote themselves to its service in the right earnest and promote gender equality.

Born at Sibsagar in Assam on 23 March, 1925 Hema Kakoti[10] is yet another woman, who actively participated in the freedom struggle. An octogenarian, Kakoti says that she got inspired to work for the nation through her father, late Durganand Kakoti and her grandmother, Sunder Bor Kakoti. Her father used her as an agent to pass on information to revolutionaries, and being young and beautiful, she was never suspected by the police. In 1942, the police ransacked her house, and arrested both her father and grandmother. However, because of her tender age, she was left alone at home. She later on became the president of Sibsagar District Congress. In 1948 she went to Wardha for training. After that she came in contact with Binoba Bhave. She toured with him on foot, propagating khadi and Bhoodan. Subsequently, she joined Kasturba Gandhi Memorial Trust and has been working there ever since as a Trust member. Till a few years ago she was working with Shakuntala Chaudhary for the empowerment of women, eradication of social evils and prohibitions. The contribution of these humble women folk speaks volumes of the abilities they possess to build a balanced and harmonious society as dreamt by Gandhiji. It is these women who could help in building up a positive attitude among the youth.

Hema Bharali[11] is another woman of substance in national liberation, whose name should be inscribed in red letters in the freedom history of Assam. She was born on 19 February 1919 at Lakhimpur. Like all great Assamese freedom fighters Hema Bharali understood her country and the world the best. A name synonymous with nationalistic pursuits, she was a great Assamese of whom every Indian can justifiably be proud. She was a women completely devoted to national and social work and never bothered about popularity power and fame. Though coming from a very protective family, the parents especially mother, wanted her to get married and lead a secured life. But like her brothers she chose instead not to turn her back on social duties. She averred that if the foundations of society were weak, it would be difficult to achieve national freedom. After her matriculation she jumped into the freedom movement. For pursuing her education and simultaneously participating in the freedom struggle, Hema Bharali joined Mahila Ashram in Wardha. Wardha was then a focal point of attraction for many prominent national leaders and freedom fighters all of which inspired her a lot. She fought many odds on her way to free her motherland from foreign yoke. She organised various processions and rallies against British imperialistic policy. Till a short while ago she was working for the tribals. She felt that the youth should have missionary zeal to work in villages.

Silent Motivators

Behind the story of these active women revolutionaries lies a small but tragic episode of the wives of some veteran freedom fighters. Women like Mina Agrawala[12], Surya Bala Bardoloi[13] and Jayanti Gogoi[14] were three women, who had virtually lived through hell, while supporting their revolutionary husbands. They pledged *swadeshi*, faced police raids and formed women groups to collect money to help the families of arrested freedom fighters.

The case study of all these women fighters reveal that they got into the freedom struggle at a very young age, largely because of the influence of the society then in ferment in a different patriotic fervour. And when they came of age, they realised the pressing need of the hour for independence and decided to choose celibacy. Rejecting the comforts and the security of a married life plunged headlong into working towards the welfare of the mankind, society and nation.

All these panegyrics, however, do not mitigate the pathos they had passed through. Research findings largely keep silent and thus speak volumes about the failure of women's participation in the patriarchal society of India. The woman wants to contribute cent percent of her energy but a gender biased society and her socialisation do not permit to put in even a portion of efforts and potential.

The history of evolution of the Indian society does not adequately recognise the efforts put in by women folk, yet much can be said about the crucial role played by women during the most significant chapter in Indian history. During the freedom struggle, when there was need of many people, the patriarchal society included women in order to swell the ranks, but forgot to record their role, thus relegating them to the background. Violence, criminalisation and character assassination - all outcomes of gender bias, curtailed their participation in all spheres of activities in the freedom struggle. This is why we are compelled to say that fifty years after independence, we have failed in redressing inequalities in education, labour, legal rights, art and literature etc. The gap is particularly galling at district level and below, when a mass movement had really brewed up. If we consider India's freedom struggle a genuine movement encompassing all sections of the society, leaving women behind and villages aside, would lead us to a lopsided presentation of history. A time of history is the revelation of heart by the participants, and before it is too late, before these real life heroes pass away, we must record their impression. Generations to come will have to work hard in establishing a genuinely equitable society. The imperative task in front of the nation is to promote and ensure equitable gender relations.

History has always been written from endocentric point of view, focusing on males and their role in building and moulding the society. This lopsided focus needs to strike a balance with gynocentric analysis, or rather provide its due to the deserving females, whose role history preserves as memorabilia. An equitable approach to analysis of events of bygone years is what we actually need in rewriting history: not endocentric or gynocentric, but men and women, shouldering equal responsibility must get equal weightage for their part played in history. Perhaps then into the next millennium India's freedom will have really a different meaning for the citizens regardless of their gender, for the role of women cannot be alienated any longer from the mainstay of India's past development.

A rich source of oral history lay buried in remote Northeastern region of the country. From Piyali to Pushpalata and from Kanaklata to Kakoti, it is an untapped wealth of memories, of oral history about India's freedom struggle in provincial Assam and its districts. The pathos and pangs of women freedom fighters are telling episodes of gender inequality. What makes these women famous is their humility, absence of profit oriented political ambition, and strong presence of a fiery desire to serve the motherland. And what differentiates them is their unique exposition in the society. It is these women who worked so to say, in the rear and on the front, thus knitting a thread of harmony in the arduous journey of national liberation. Yet their efforts remain largely remain unwritten. Writing about them and their activities is a salutary tribute to the real icons of our independence.

References

1. The author worked in the Northeast between 2000-02 during the summer breaks to collect data on women freedom fighters of the region. This article is based on observations and interviews.
2. Anil Dutta Mishra, *Gender Perspective*, Radha Publication, New Delhi, 1998, p.5.
3. Bibekanand Das and L.N. Das, *The Feminine Gender*, Manak Publication, New Delhi, 1995, p.138.
4. Meera Kosambi, (ed) *Women Oppression in the Public Gaze*, RCWS, SNDT University, 1994, p.3.
5. Extracted from Guwahati University Journal, 1998, pp. 1-3.
6. Dipti Sharma and Anuradha Dutta, *Women's role in the Freedom Struggle in Assam*, 1998.
7. Gopinath Bardoloi Committee Report, also interview with Swaranlata Mohanto at Tezpur in Sonitpur district on 2 June 2001 at her residence. Her contribution to the freedom struggle was referred to by Satish Chandra Kakoti, an eminent freedom fighter, during his interview on 28 May, 2001at his residence in Basistha Chariali, Guwahati in Assam.
8. (i) Pushpalata Das, *Asohajog Andolanat Narir Abadan* (Manuscript in Assamese), (ii) See O.K. Das, *Divansmriti*, Guwahati, 1938, p-179, iii) Interview with Pushpalata Das on 10 June 2001 at her residence in Kala Pahar in Guwahati, in Assam.

9. Interview with Pramila Barua on 17 June 2000 at her residence in Tezpur Darrang Road, Assam.
10. Interview with Hema Kakoti on 25 June 2000 at her residence in Kasturba Gandhi Memorial Trust at Guwahati, in Assam.
11. Interview with Hema Bharali on 26 June 2000 at her residence in Pub Saraniya in Guwahati, Assam.
12. Interview with Mina Agrawala on 18 June 2000 at her residence at Tezpur in Sonitpur district of Assam.
13. Interview with Suryabala Bardoloi on 25 June 2000 at her residence in Guwahati.
14. Interview with Jayanti Gogoi on 26 June 2000 at her residence at Bamuni Press .

17

New Morality and Women's Liberation in Western India

Jaswandi Wamburkar Utagikar

There is a tendency among historians to separate the women's history of modern period into watertight compartments of nineteenth century and twentieth century. The history of nineteenth century was marked by the women's reform movement initiated mostly by men and centered around the eradication of various social evils such as female infanticide, child-marriage, sati, ban on widow remarriage, tonsuring of women's head, and ban on female education and so on. The women's history of the first half of the twentieth century is subsumed under the carpet of the Indian National Movement. It is believed that the movement received a serious setback in the first two decades popularly known as 'Tilak-era' and received a boost in the Gandhian-era. The contribution of women either in the working class movement or peasant movement or Gandhian movement has been widely written upon by historians though large areas are still unexplored.[1] This is known as contributory history.[2] However, the women's reform movement reached new horizons in the first half of the twentieth century in Western India. An attempt has been made in this paper to study the new trends, shifts, and paradigm of the women's liberation movement in the given period. Various articles traced in the contemporary newspapers or magazines have been used as primary source-materials in this paper.[3]

Women and Education

The beginning of twentieth century witnessed a steady progress in female education, which was no doubt the legacy of nineteenth century women's reform movement. The educational experiments of the nineteenth century produced a 'new woman' who was capable of shaping her own future. Pandita Ramabai[4] established Sharada Sadan in 1889 at Mumbai, which was shifted to Kedgaon in 1898 due to space constraints. Sharada Sadan was a home for the destitute and orphan women. It was named after its first student Sharda Gadre. It gave shelter and training to nearly two thousand women in Ramabai's reign.

Ramabai Ranade[5] started Hindu Ladies Social and Literary club in 1894 to give training to women for Marathi language, General knowledge, English language and sewing etc. She established the Sevasadan in 1908 with nearly 700 women students on roll in its first seven years. Branches of Pune Sevasadan spread in few years to Mumbai, Satara, Solapur, Ahmednagar and so on. Sevasadan never aimed at making woman merely a better housewife but it aimed at her economic independence. In 1924, nearly 1000 women were on the rolls of Sevasadan.

Vitthal Ramji Shinde[6] and his sister Janakka Shinde started Depressed Class Mission Society of India in 1906 where Janakka used to teach girls from depressed classes. Vitthal Ramji Shinde launched a movement against the evil practice of Devdasi in Hindu community. Untouchable women from Jejuri, Tuljapur, Kumath, Shirasi, etc. used to be dedicated to God as Murali, Jogtin, Bhavin, Basavi, which are the different forms of Devdasi. This evil practice had the sanction of religion. It was nothing but a legalized prostitution. He organized a conference in Mumbai for the eradication of the custom of Murali in 1911. He wrote articles about the history of Devdasi practice in India to get public support for his movement. He was also instrumental in the movement for making primary education compulsory for women.

Dhondo Keshav Karve[7] established the first Women's University in India in 1916 known as S.N.D.T. Women's University. Various branches were opened at Pune, Mumbai Satara, Solapur, Belgaum, etc. Though Karve was of the opinion that home was the primary sphere of activity for women, girls enjoyed free atmosphere in the university that gave rise to new aspirations and new consciousness among them. Malati Bedekar in an interview had narrated the manner in which the teachers such as Vaman Malhar Joshi and D.K Karve used to raise new questions in the group discussions held in the classrooms that kindled new awareness in them.[8] Women started thinking of building new careers for themselves. Parvatibai Athavale in her autobiography beautifully narrated such feelings: "Education awakened my mind. I determined on carrying out my ideal. And for this purpose I decided to give my whole life to the service of the Widow's Home."[9] Vibhavari Shirurkar in her father's biography 'Kharemaster'[10] narrated that though tonsuring of head was banned by law, an unshorn widow hardly existed at that time. However at D.K. Karve's Hingane Streeshikshansanstha, there were equal numbers of shorn and unshorn widows. It was a very rebellious act for that period.

It was also a period when women started showing extraordinary achievements in the field of higher education.[11] Kamalabai Deshpande a student of Women's University completed her Ph.D. at University of Prague under the able guidance of well-known Sanskrit scholar, Winternitz. Krishnabai Mote went to England to complete a diploma in Social work from London School of Sociology in 1932. Seetabai Annegiri received a research fellowship at the Neels College in America. Iravati Karve completed her Ph.D. in anthropology in Germany. She later on became the registrar of the Women's University. Shakuntala Paranjpe went to Cambridge for further education. Seetabai Paramanand, a student of Hujurpaga School went to Oxford University and completed her Ph.D. on the theme 'The Position of Women in Ancient India as Represented in the Dharmashastras.'

Women and Work

Another factor which brought a sea change in women's lives was women's entry in the public sphere, though their number was small and the fields of work were also limited to education and medicine. The lower class women due to the economic pressures had already started working in either farm-fields or factories. However there was always a social taboo to work for the middle class women and the higher caste women. Women had always been looked upon as wives and mothers in the Victorian value-structure.

Women entered various fields and crossed the boundaries of home for the first time, which created a new confidence and new consciousness in them. Women started working as teachers in schools, nurses and doctors, clerks in government offices. At the initial stage the society was for the economic independence of only widows. But slowly even unmarried or married women started entering public sphere. Students of Women's University were offered jobs working in the university itself. Parvatibai Athavale started assisting D. K. Karve in the Widow's Home. Vibhavari Shirurkar and Geeta Sane started working as teachers in the Women's University at Pune. Various women started coaching classes for sewing, home management, cooking classes etc for women.

Though women entered the public arena, the society and the government had a conventional outlook towards it. Kusumavati Deshpande, a graduate in English literature, applied for the post of lecturer in Morris College at Nagpur, but the C.P and Berar government withheld her application.[12] This issue was taken up by various journals in Maharashtra and finally her application was accepted and later on, she was selected for the post of lecturer in the college. This was a triumph of progressive journalism as well as public opinion. This event shows a shift in the attitudes of the society towards women.

The first three decades of twentieth century witnessed a rise and fall of nearly three hundred and fifty periodicals in Maharashtra. Many magazines or periodicals were meant for women. Even in the regular newspapers or magazines there used to be columns for women. Various educated women got absorbed in various magazines or newspaper companies as clerks, writers, typists etc. Women took over even as editors of various magazines such as 'Aryagruhini' (1925), 'Gruhalakshmi' (1927), 'Saraswati' (1928), 'Manorama' (1929), 'Stree' (1930), 'Mahila' (1933) and 'Janani' (1933).[13]

Another factor that gave impetus to women's employment was the First World War in (1914-1948) and the Second World War (1939-1945). The war situation compelled men to go to war, which in turn gave opportunities to women to work in the public sphere and for the increased production in the country. This gave her a new insight about her own potential. Such confidence resulted in various journalistic expressions.

Dr. Saibai Ranade[14] in her article 'Women and Vocational Education' had expressed the opinion that women should not feel that they were inferior to men in any respect. She had suggested an Eight-point programme for the women aspirants for entry in the business world. This programme was based on one American business woman's advice.

Arundhati Apte[15] in her article 'Women's competition in Men's Sector' identified five fields as 'sphere of men' – literature, service sector, religious education, social work and politics. She made a review of women's contribution to literature from Mahadamba to Sarojini Naidu. However, she criticized the writings, and said that women had not produced revolutionary literature so far. In her opinion, it was very self-centered.

She opined that women were potentially better teachers due to their peace loving and caring nature as compared to men who had masculine characteristics by nature such as short temper, rationalism and pragmatism. Women were born mothers and therefore they were tolerant, mentally controlled, caring. She felt that physically women were weaker to men and therefore they should not work in factories or industries. Another reason put forth by her was the intermixing of men and women at the workplace could lead to immoral practices among them. She welcomed white-collar jobs like typing, telephone-offices, telegraph offices, as doctors, nurses, cinema or theatre for women. She believed that women should come forward to teach religious education. Women should also come forward for the modernization of the villages and for the upliftment of the untouchables.

She thought that history had proved that women were always in the forefront of politics. She welcomed the emergence of new women on the horizon of politics, who wanted to dedicate their lives for the nation. In a nutshell, she considered that women were capable of competing with men in all spheres of life and therefore women should enter various new fields without hesitation.

Seetabai Sawant[16] in her article 'World War and Womenfolk' narrated the role of women in times of war. Women had assisted men from ancient periods during war conditions without expecting any returns. However during the First World War, there was a growing demand for women to assist men on various fronts. The suffragette movement was at its peak and taking advantage of the situation, the women's movement kept their demand of voting rights for women to the forefront. However, the author did not like this opportunist stand taken by the leaders of the women's movement.

As a result of the war conditions women occupied various fields that were kept exclusively for men in Europe. Women started working in government offices, hospitals, and factories, which shattered the age-old myth that home was the primary sphere for women. It built up new confidence in them. This change gave a boost to the women's movement in Europe. On the one hand, woman became aware of her innate potential, but on the other, she was disillusioned by the various taboos or restrictions kept on her by social norms for ages. She started raising new questions about women's rights.

Ironically, the author had targeted this 'new cult of women' and held them responsible for the moral breakdown of the society. She believed that the economically independent women misused their freedom and therefore, women's character was in danger. She warned the Indian women to remain aloof from such evil effects of the war. She felt that the pride and prestige of India could be retained only as long as Indian woman was pure and virtuous. However, the author did not address a single word about men's character or morality. She also did not seem to be aware of the war situations that forced women to satisfy the sexual needs of the soldiers on the war-front. She did not take any pains to dig out the root of the problem - the capitalist system forcing nations to war.

Durga Khote[17] in her article 'My Steps in Film Industry' narrated in what manner the middle class woman had to support her family in the changing situations. She suggested that cinema was one of the respectable fields suitable for such needy women. According to her, people had wrong notions about cinema. They looked down upon cinema and feared that woman's entry in cinema would lead to her moral degradation. But she felt that it was a very dignified source of income. Durga Khote concluded her article with very significant remarks. She said that every human being was gifted with a personality and that was the essence of one's identity. Come what may, one must try to retain one's personality. This is a rare kind of confidence that had been reflected in women's writing.

Saraswatibai Kirloskar's[18] article 'Women and Child Labor in Uncontrolled Business' was in origin a lecture delivered at the Fifth Women's Council gathering held on 9th February 1940 at Mumbai. The author put forth the plea of the working class women. She narrated the miserable conditions under which women worked and how the factory owner or handloom owner exploited them. She identified the two-fold exploitation of these women, firstly, at the hands of the factory owner, and secondly, at the hands of the patriarchy. The woman worker worked at the factory for 14 hours a day and then she was supposed to cook and look after children. Moreover she had to face various kinds of allegations laid on her character by the husband and members in the family. The author suggested that the government should make legal provision for one and half month's salaried maternity leave for these women. Finally, she expressed the belief that a nation could be free in the real sense only when the slavery of the workers would come to an end.

Shridhar Vyankatesh Ketkar[19] in his article 'Economic Independence of Women and Transformation in Society' made an attempt to study the various factors responsible for the secondary position of women in society. In his opinion, though women's entry into public fields had made a marginal impact on women's lives, the patriarchal social-structure could not be completely uprooted. According to him though women worked either in fields or factories their physical strength could never match to that of men. The middle class women worked either as doctors or nurses or businesswomen or clerk, but they had their own limitations as nature had conferred upon them the responsibility of childbirth and child rearing. This reproductive capacity would always remain as an obstacle in her growth and development. As far as widows and spinsters were concerned, the author was of the opinion that these women always remained psychologically affected because they were deprived of the joys and happiness one got from family and marriage. Such psychologically unsatisfied women could not give their complete potential and therefore could not compete with men in public sphere. Thus married or unmarried, poor or middleclass, women would remain behind men in public sphere. Therefore, the position of women dependant on men would always remain secondary in patriarchal system and these were the limitations created by nature in man-woman equality.

At the end of the article, the author ironically assured society not to worry about any kind of drastic change in women's position. S.V. Ketkar was known for bringing an encyclopedia for the first time in Marathi. He married a European woman, Kohan known as Sheelavati Ketkar. He was known as a great scholar and well read person in those days. It would perhaps be audacious to conclude that the he was not aware of the contemporary birth-control movement which brought a radical change in the lives of the women. That women were physically weaker than men was a myth which carried substantial weightage in those days. In fact, the rise of capitalism had minimized the importance of masculine power. The author apparently echoed the psychology of men folk who might have felt insecure due to the growing importance of women in public sphere. This change might have shattered the myth of male superiority over women and have become instrumental in breaking the age-old patriarchal male-domination in the society.

Pramilabai Talwalkar[20] in her article 'Provision for Future' stressed the dire need of provision of insurance for women. She began by outlining the miserable condition of a woman after her husband's death. As the joint family system had been replaced by the nuclear family, some provision for her future economic well being was the need of the hour. However, she regretted that most women either did not take it seriously or were not aware of such insurance provision. She pleaded that every girl at the time of her wedding should get such insurance either from her natal place or from her husband. She made mention of few women such as Miss Zutsi, Miss Arubai, Renuka Gupta and Jyotirmayi Ganguly who were working with insurance companies. This shows the growing consciousness among women about their own economic security.

Malati Bakve[21] in her article 'Whether women should be insured?' expressed exactly the opposite opinion as to whether women should be insured. She seemed to be suspicious about how far women would get the benefits from such a provision. She felt that unless the outlook of society towards women changed, such kind of provisions would prove futile. She suspected that a husband might feel that his wife should die since then only he would get the monetary benefits from the insurance company. She believed that the working class women, in particular, should never go for any such insurance since their male counterparts would always have an eye on their money. She firmly believed that men were illiterate, addicted and womanizers. So, insurance would put the woman's life in unnecessary danger.

Sexual Revolution in the West[22]

Though various material changes were responsible for the rise of a 'new woman' in society, the ideological impact of various new trends in the west also had an impact on the indigenous mind. The twentieth century was a period of 'sexual revolution' in the west. Linda Gordon defined 'sexual revolution' as reproductive self-determination along with unlimited sexual indulgence. With the beginning of the twentieth century, a new cult of intellectuals and reformers arose in Europe and America, who were greatly influenced by the European sexual theorists. Nineteenth century Liberalism had fought for man-woman equality. This 'new morality' fought for the 'sexual and economic rights' of women. Most of the sex theorists were pro-feminist and were of the opinion that a woman could not be truly liberated until she achieved sexual liberation. There were sex-theorists such as Havelock Ellis, Edward Carpenter, and Ellen Key who were known as 'new moralists'.

It was an era of birth control in the West and America. The Liberal feminism advocated man-woman equality. However, middle class women in the capitalist mode of production were economically dependent on either the husband or the family or the patriarch. The Victorian value structure underlined the home as the primary sphere of women's activity. She had no right over her own body. Various thinkers such as Nolton, Havelock Ellis supported woman's rights to her body. They believed that a woman should have a right to decide when and how many children she should have. She should also be free from the sexual exploitation done within marriage system. In 'Origin of State, Private Property and the Family', published in 1884, Frederick Engels made an attempt to prove that the origin of state, private property and the institution of marriage-system are correlated to each other. Women's sexual as well as economic enslavement began with the rise of marriage as a social institution. Most of the twentieth century socialist thinkers were of the opinion that a goal of socialism could not be achieved unless class of woman was free and marriage-system should be abolished to achieve the actual freedom of a woman.

Francis Leps, Richard Carlyle, George Drissdel, Charles Bradlow and Annie Besant initiated the birth control movement in Europe in nineteenth century. Margaret Sanger was the pioneer of the birth control movement in America.[23] She also wrote various books on birth control and sex education.[24]

Bertrand Russell published his book, 'Marriage and Morals' in 1929.[25] He came up with a new sexual morality, which was not acceptable to the conventional society. He was the champion of sexual freedom of a human being. In his opinion, birth control techniques had revolutionized the sexual morality. Reproduction and sexual activity were to be treated as two separate activities. In his opinion true love should be the only basis of marriage system. He advocated trial marriage. The new sexual morality should be based on mutual consent. Woman became the permanent slave of her husband in a marriage system due to her economic dependence on him. He considered prostitution as equally immoral since it forced woman to engage in sexual activity for her livelihood. He advocated free extra-marital relations since he believed monogamy was unnatural. He advocated free sex education for the healthy growth of the adolescents.

Women and Era of New Morality

The post-1920's witnessed a radical shift in writings on new morality among leading intellectuals and social reformers in Western India. They were greatly influenced by Western sexual theorists such as Havelock Ellis, Freud, Bertrand Russell and others. This period is known as an era of "*Navmatawad*" (new morality) in the history of Western India.[26] Women started raising new questions regarding women's economic and sexual rights. The new magazines such as 'Stree', 'Samajswasth', 'Janani', 'Savai Jeevan', 'Yauvan' and 'Rati' started addressing issues concerning contraception, abortion, sexual health and women's sexual problems.[27] Women writers came forward and boldly expressed their views about the discrepancies between men and women in sexual morality, and sexual harassment of women in the marriage-system. They also challenged the custom of Devdasi and the issue of prostitution in India.

The child-marriage was replaced by adult-marriage. A single adult career-oriented woman became a regular sight in the society. Working women had to stay away from their family, and created a new space for themselves in society.[28]

The independent stay of such working women created a new confidence in them. It gave them a space where there was very little interference of either the family members or relatives. Their free interaction with men at work place was an entirely new experience for them. Many such free interactions resulted in love marriages, a few of which became very controversial.[29]

The 'new women' also took up issues pertaining to women's lives such as prostitution, law of divorce, right of inheritance, law of abortion, voting-right for women, problems of working class women and so on. Many men also became instrumental in promoting this movement. R. D. Karve, son of D. K. Karve started the first centre for family planning and for selling contraceptive devices in 1921.[30] It was perhaps the first centre of its kind not only in India but also in Asia. He started a monthly magazine 'Samajswasth' from July 1927.[31] 'Savai Jeevan' was another periodical that was dedicated to issues dealing with sex. Its sub-title was 'the only magazine satisfying the quest for sex-knowledge'. Its first editor was a woman named Shobhana.

V.K. Rajwade published his magnum opus 'The History of Indian Marriage-System'. The ancient work of Vatsyayan named 'Kamasutra' (the science of romance) was published by Mr. Tolawalkar with the title *'Ratishashtrameemansa'* in 1934. The well known author, Shridhar Vyankatesh Ketkar wrote an introduction to this book in which he appreciated the efforts of the editor of this book to unite the ancient Indian sexology as well as western modern sexology.[32] Anant Kanekar translated 'Marriage and Morals' into Marathi and published it with the title *"Raselaneetee"* in 1941. V. K. Kirloskar translated Frederick Engels' book, 'Origin of State, Private Property and the Family' into Marathi with the title *"Vivahsansthecha Itihas"* in 1937.

Sex Education

Shakuntala Paranjpe[33] delivered a lecture at the Sex Science Conference in 1942. She started assisting R.D. Karve in the birth-control movement from 1937. She wrote various articles on issues related to contraception, family planning, sex education in various journals such as Dhyanprakash, Sawai Jeevan, Samajswasth, and Jeevan, to name a few. People had many misconceptions about family planning methods. Some orthodox people deliberately used to oppose family planning. Shakuntala Paranjape at the very outset of the lecture expressed the two-fold aspects of the birth-control movement: firstly, to satisfy ones sexual desire without any harm to the body and secondly to secure intelligent and healthy progeny. According to her, birth control aimed to have limited but healthy and brave progeny rather than too many weak and unhealthy children. She emphasized that it would be wrong to consider birth control a means for excessive sexual indulgence. She argued that a device could never in itself be good or bad, rather it depended upon the intellect of the user. She made a fiery attack on the men folk of India who kept the womenfolk in perpetual ignorance for ages and confined their roles to housekeeping and child rearing. Many women faced death due to recurring pregnancies. She believed that the birth-control devices could give a new life to women. She condemned Keshavshastri, who seemed to have spoken against contraception in the conference, openly.

Shakuntala Paranjpe[34] in her article 'Mummy where does the Baby come from?' stressed the importance of sex education. She criticized the attitude of the parents who did not quench the thirst for knowledge of their children about sex issues. She condemned the puritan Indian society which failed to create a health environment in the family. She felt that nudity was natural and it should be followed to some extent at least to give sex education and to create a healthy outlook in children. She warned that if parents failed to answer their queries, children would have to search for another source of knowledge outside the home, which might prove dangerous to them.

Indirabai Gadre[35] in her article 'Remedy for the Fallen Woman and Duties of Elderly People' discussed the various factors responsible for the moral degradation of a woman. Firstly, she stated that the quest of children about sex issues was not satisfied in the family and so, they had to find out a way outside the home that might take them on wrong path. According to her, the second factor was the sexual exploitation of women done by men in the manner Mughals or Muslims used to do. She seemed to be carrying the burden of the 'myth of the golden age.'[36] Thirdly, she felt that custom of child marriage and taboo on widow remarriage were considerably responsible for the moral degradation of women since it would be hard to suppress the natural instincts in one's youth.

The author considered that the entire education system was so faulty that though a girl studied till post-graduation, no coverage was given to sex education in the syllabi. She was discouraged from raising inconvenient questions in the family too. She felt sad that excessive secrecy was maintained about reproduction, which was a natural phenomenon upon which the future of the whole mankind was dependent. She opined that suppression was the vital cause of the degeneration of women and therefore fewer restrictions should be kept on the movements of girls.

Women and Sex Morality

The author of the article, 'Widow and Widower'[37] kept her name secret, and only referred to herself as 'a live widow'. This article is a very bold expression on the part of a widow. Though the widow-remarriage movement had gained momentum in Western India, only child-widows used to get married and nobody used to think about the middle-aged widows and their sorrows. The author was a middle-aged widow who was educated and rich who had the sole responsibility of her children. She vehemently criticized the double standards of the society about the social norms about a widow and a widower. She questioned why the society remained sympathetic towards a widower of the age of 40, who could think of second marriage and why the same society never showed sympathy to a widow of 30, as if a woman did not have any strong natural desires. Rather, society considered that it was her prime duty to look after her children and she should not even think of any other man. She asserted that, though man and woman were made up of the same soil, society had different sets of rules for them. She further asserted that monogamy was artificial both for men and women and regarded them as cultural constructs partial to men.

The author openly stated that though she looked after her children properly, her heart craved for a life-partner at times and she had to suppress her emotions due to wrong social practices. A widower was generally advised to keep a mistress and yet live a respectful life to avoid any inconvenience or miseries of his children that might be caused on account of a stepmother. But a widow was considered as "immoral" if she followed such a practice. She asserted that she might go for such an option if the conditions were favourable and she would not feel bad about it.

Kamla[38] in her article 'New Morality and Reform' took the side of the new moralists. She believed that the change that had occurred, that economically independent women preferred to remain unmarried, should be considered as a sign of progress of society. Arguing that the natural instincts of human beings were as old as the human race itself, she approved of the new moralists, who taught society to look at them from a new viewpoint, so as to understand the evil effects of suppressing the natural desires.

Kumudini Prabhavalkar[39] in her article 'Mr. Jadhav's New Bill' criticized Mr. Jadhav's bill for abortion. According to the Indian Penal Code in 1933, abortion was not a crime by law, if it was saving the life of a woman. Mr. Jadhav wanted to reform this act by adding a clause to it: abortion should not be considered as a crime as long as it did not cause any physical, social or economic harm. The author affirmed that nature had become favourable to men and it had thrown the responsibility of retaining the moral standards of society on women. She objected the bill on two grounds: firstly, women would misuse this law for all immoral practices. Secondly, such disgraced women would never be acceptable in society. She disapproved of this law on economic grounds as well. According to her, the woman might not be able to afford to look after a child born out of such illegal relationship. However, the author did not talk about the traumatic conditions under which a raped woman had to live her entire life with forced motherhood. The author did not blame the man who also must be considered equally responsible for the rearing of the offspring and the system which allowed him to easily escape from such responsibility. The author did not bother to raise the question as to why only a woman had to face the consequences of one such deed for the whole of her life. She was not puzzled about the double standards of the society about men and women's sexual behaviour. She did not question as to why it was only womenfolk who were held responsible for the moral breakdown of the society and not the men.

Shridhar Vyankatesh Ketkar[40] in his article 'One parameter of Sexual Morality for Men and Women and its Feasibility' had avowed that it would be impossible to bring man-woman equality into reality. He said that though women had gradually become self-employed, many of them would remain dependent on their husbands. Economy in his opinion was the basis of any social structure. It would be difficult to have similar sexual moral standards for men and women in a society where women on a large scale were dependant on men. Men in the patriarchal society would always expect total loyalty from their life partners. Secondly, since nature had gifted women with reproductive capacity, it would be difficult for her to hide her sexual indulgence. And that was why gender disparity would be eternal as far as sexual morality was concerned.

It would be perhaps ridiculous to conclude that a well read scholar like Ketkar was not aware of the invention of the contraceptive measures that had brought a sea change in a woman's life. Ketkar seemed to have taken up this issue in a very superficial manner. A sociologist like him should have made an attempt to study the grass root causes of the gender discrimination regarding sexual morality. Ketkar appears to be representing the feelings of the contemporary men folk who wanted reform at one hand but were disillusioned to see the breakdown of the traditional patriarchal value structure on the other.

Dr.V. K. Joshi[41] in his article 'What should we do then?' related the story of a woman named Chapala who became a victim of male lust and was pregnant. This story was in the form of a conversation between her and her friend Abhay who wished to marry her and thereby give her a new life. It was a period when abortion was considered as a serious crime unless it had been done to save the life of the concerned woman. They finally resorted to aborting the unwanted child, knowing that they might have to face a legal action. Surprisingly, the court gave the verdict in favour of the woman. The judge interpreted the law to say that saving a woman did not mean just keeping her alive. Rather, if pregnancy was causing any harm to her mental as well as her physical well-being, abortion done in such a situation could not be considered as a crime. Dr. Joshi had made an attempt in this article to create public sympathy for such an unfortunate woman.

Women and Prostitution

Rajaratna Joshi[42] in his article 'An Incurable disease Veiled by the Society' made a scientific study of the age-old practice of prostitution. He strove to find out the foundation of the custom of prostitution. It was the only source to fulfil their sexual needs for the married men or widower. Many married men went to prostitutes, as they were sexually not happy with their wives. As far as women were concerned, most of the women were lured by men and were forced to accept prostitution. The author held the social system responsible for compelling women to enter this profession. Widow remarriage was not widespread though it was acceptable by law. Disgraced women or unmarried mothers became so unacceptable in society that they were left with no option other than prostitution. Once these women were caught in such a trap, they could never come out. He criticized the society for treating the prostitutes as 'untouchables'. The new moralists such as Bertrand Russell and Havelock Ellis had suggested that free man-woman relationship based on mutual consent was the sole remedy for the eradication of prostitution. However, the author felt that the remedy was more dangerous than the disease itself. He disagreed that prostitution was the product of capitalism, since prostitution was as age-old custom. He suggested that the remedy adopted by Russia for the upliftment of the prostitutes should be followed in India. Russia had opened up prophylactoria for the prostitutes and they had been given a new source of income. Many of them married somebody and started a new life. The author made a plea to the readers to treat the prostitutes as human beings and be sympathetic towards them.

'Escape from the Clutches of Maragi'[43] is an article by Anandibai Kirloskar on the miserable plea of the prostitutes. She interviewed various women who were forced into prostitution, and found out was that most of the women were brought either forcibly or cunningly into the trap. She also found out that prostitution was a highly systematized business that made the escape of these women impossible. She narrated a story of a brave woman who became instrumental in the escape of almost 70 to 75 prostitutes from the clutches of Maragi, the owner of the brothel. However, the future of these women was dark since there was no provision for their rehabilitation. What is striking about this article is that the author had pleaded that women look at the prostitutes as their own sisters and not as 'other women'. They were not born prostitutes, in fact they were the worst victims of the social system and so, they should be looked at from a humanitarian attitude. This kind of consciousness has been rarely sighted in the writings of the upper caste women.

Thus, the Women's liberation movement ran parallel with the Indian National Movement in the first half of the twentieth century. The failure of the national movement lies in the fact that it remained deaf to the women's voices that sought to galvanize public opinion on the gender bias of society. Gender issues were sidetracked for the primacy of the struggle for independence.

References

1. Following are some of the works:
   Rohini Gavanakar, *Marathi Streeshakteeche Rajakarani Roop*, Aditya Prakashan, 1986.
   Urmila Pawar and Meenakshi Moon, *Amhihi Itihas Ghadavala*, Mumbai, Stree Uwacha Prakashan, 1989.
   Y. D. Phadke, *Nahi Cheera Nahi Panati*, Pune, Shreevidya Prakashan, 2000.
2. Gerda Lerner, *The Majority Finds Its Past*, New York, OUP, 1979, p. 146.
3. Eighteen articles published in various contemporary magazines have been used in this paper as primary source material. For the selection of the articles thematic approach has been adopted. Almost eleven articles have been located in various contemporary magazines and received at Dadar Marathi Granthasangrahalaya, Mumbai. Remaining seven articles have been taken from the following edited work:
   Dr. Swati Karve (Ed.) *Stree Vikasachya Paulkhuna*, Pune, Pratima Prakashan, 2003.
4. For all informative details please see Uma Chakravarti, *Rewriting History: the Life and Times of Pandita Ramabai*, New Delhi, Kali For Women, 1998.
5. For all informative details please see Ramabai Ranade, *Amachya Ayushyatil Kahi athavani*, Mumbai, Anubhav Publication, 1993. (First published in 1910).
6. For more details please see Tanaji Thombare, *Maharshi Vitthal Ramaji Shinde Yanchya Rajakiya va Samajik Chalavali*, Mumbai, Lokvangamay Gruha, 1999.
7. For all informative details please see Dhondo Keshav Karve, *Atmavrutt va Charitra*, Pune, Hingane Stree Shikshan Sanstha, 1958.

8. Malati Bedekar cited in Vinaya Khadapekar, *Streeswatantryavadini. Visavya Shatakatil Parivartan*, Mumbai, Popular Prakashan, 1991, p. 165.
9. Parvati Athavale, *My Story. The Autobiography of a Hindu Widow,* (translated by Rev. Justin E. Abbott), London, G. P. Putnam's Sons, 1930, P.30.
10. Vibhavari Shirurkar, *Kharemaster* (translated from Marathi by Yashodhara Maitra), Calcutta, Stree, 1998, P. 81.
11. For all informative details please see Abaji Vishwanath Modak, *Hingane Stree Shikshan Sansthechi Sath Varshe*, Pune, Hingane Stree Shikshan Sanstha, 1956.
12. Sudha Gogte, *Status Of Woman Reflected in Marathi Media*, Pune, Shubhada Saraswat Publications Pvt. Ltd., 1988, p. 39.
13. Vinaya Khadapekar, Op. cit, P. 4.
4. Dr. Saibai Ranade, "Striya va Dhandeshikshan", *Gruhalaksmi*, October 1927, cited in Dr. Swati Karve (Ed.) *Stree Vikasachya Paulkhuna*, Pune, Pratima Prakashan, 2003,p p. 202-204.
15. Arundhati Apte, "Purushanche Vyavaharat Striyanchi Spardha", *Mahila,* July 1933 cited in Swati Karve, Op. cit, pp. 212-217.
16. Seetabai Sawant, "Mahayudhha ani Mahilavarga," *Gruhiniratnamala*, March-April 1919, Ibid. pp. 183-189.
17. Durga Khote, " Chitrapatasrushtitil Maze Paul", *Mauj*, Film Silver Jubilee Special Issue, 1939, Ibid, pp. 239-243.
18. Saraswatibai Kirloskar, "Aniyantrit Dhandyat Rabanarya Striya va Mule", *Stree*, March 1940, p.p. 546-549.
19. Shreedhar Vyankatesh Ketkar, "Striyanche arthik swatantrya ani Samajache Rupantar", *Stree*, March 1933, p.p. 393-396.
20. Pramilabai Talwalkar, "Provision for Future", *Stree*, July, 1933,p. p.651-652.
21. Malati Bakve, "Striyani Vima Utaravava Kai", *Stree*, August 1941,p.30.
22. Linda Gordon, *Woman's Body, Woman's Right, Birth Control in America*, Penguin Books, 1990, (First published in 1974), p.p.183-242.
23. Virginia Coigney, *Margaret Sanger: Rebel with a Cause*, New York, Doubleday and Co., 1969.
24. Margaret Sanger wrote the books: 'The case of Birth Control' in 1917, 'Woman and the New Race' in 1920, 'New Morality and Birth Control' in 1922, 'Happiness in Marriage' in 1926 and 'Motherhood in Bondage' in 1928.
25. Bertrand Russell, *Marriage and Morals*, London, George Allen and Unwin Ltd., 1952 (First published in 1929).

26. G. M. Kulkarni, V. D. Kulkarni (Eds.), *Marathi Vangamayacha Itihas*, Vol. VI, Part I, Pune, Maharashtra Sahitya Parishad, 1988, pp.182-187.
27. Manda Khandage et. al., *Stree Sahityacha Magova*, Vol. I, Sahityapremi Bhagini Mandal, Pune, 2002, p.p. 14-19.
28. Women such as Malatibai Dedekar, Shantabai Bapat, Venutain Panse, Chandrabai Karnataki, Sulabha Panandikar remained unmarried for their entire lives for the sake of career. A well-known writer of those days, Balutai Khare was offered a job at Amaravati and her parents were reluctant to send her at such a distant place. However, finally she accepted that challenge. Balutai Khare rejected Mr. Purandare, a lawyer since he disapproved her to seek help from anybody, in her research except him. She realized that he would control her entire existence if she would marry him and therefore she broke the relationship with him. She refused to marry a man who asked for a dowry. Finally she married Vishram Bedekar at the age of 33, which was a love marriage. Kusumavati Deshpande, a Cambridge returned scholar from Pune stayed at Nagpur for the sake of job.
29. Krishnabai Mote married Haribhao Mote at the age of 32. It was a love marriage. Sakuntala Paranjpe married Yura Sleptjaz, a Russian painter. She divorced him in 1937 and came back to India. Mailini Panandikar, granddaughter of Dr. R.G. Bhandarkar married a Muslim man named Gulabkhan. Geeta Sane married Narsingh Dhagamwar. She worked as vice-principal for few years in a college at Meerut.
30. Y. D. Phadke, *R. D. Karve*, Mumbai, H. V. Mote Prakashan, 1981.
31. He published the first book on contraception in 1923. He introduced various western writers to the society such as Dr. Norman Hayer, Judge Lindse, Bertrand Russell, Dr. Robinson, Havelock Ellis, Freud and their views on different issues such as contraception, marriage system and its future, morality regarding marriage, sex and health and so on. It was noteworthy that eleven women were the subscribers of Samajswasth. Due to its increasing popularity, he published his book in Hindi and Gujarati as well. He touched upon various themes such as venereal diseases, abortion, celibacy, non-vegetarianism, prostitution, problem of population, sex education, and the science of sex.
32. Y. D. Phadke (Ed.) *Ketkar Lekhsangrah*, New Delhi, Sahitya Academy, 1977, p. 182.
33. Shakuntala Paranjpe, "Laingik Vidhyan Parishad, (Bhashan)" *Sawai Jeevan*, February, 1942, Cited in Swati Karve, *op.cit.*, pp. 255-257.

34. Shakuntala Paranjpe, "Aai Bal Kothun Aal?", *Jeevan*, March 1941, pp. 21-25.
35. Indirabai Gadre, "Stripatananivarak Upay va Vadil Manasanche Kartavya", *Gruhalakshmi,* June 1928, cited in Swati Karve, *op.cit.*, pp. 138-144.
36. The ideology of liberalism provided the philosophical foundation to the women's reform movement of the nineteenth century. However it was not the sheer duplication of Western liberal feminism. The newly educated reformers always had the fear of the 'loss of identity' by the total westernization of the Indian tradition. An attempt was made to unload the burden of the 'low status of Indian women' by the creation of the 'myth of the golden age'. That Indian woman was honoured with very high status in Vedic period which reached its pinnacle in the Gupta period and it was the Muslim rule which should be held responsible for its degeneration was not a truism.
37. Not mentioned, "Vidhur ani Vidhava", *Yashawant*, September 1942, *Ibid.*, pp. 145-150.
38. Kamala, "Navmatawad va Sudharana", *Navi Gruhalakshmi*, September 1928, *Ibid.*, pp. 205-211.
39. Kumudini Prabhavalkar, "Na Jadhav Yanche Nave Bill", *Mahila*, August 1933, Ibid, pp. 218-221.
40. Shreedhar Vyankatesh Ketkar, "Stree-purushans Aaindriyaneeteeche Ekacha Pariman va Tyachi Shakyashakyata", *Stree*, July, 1933, pp. 645-646.
41 V.K. Joshi, "Mag Amhi Kai Karave?", *Stree*, September 1940, pp. 249-252.
42. V. V. Joshi, "Samajane Zakun Thevalela Asadhya Rog", *Stree*, March 1939, pp. 551-555.
43. Anandibai Kirloskar, "Marageechya Magaramithitun Sutaka", *Stree*, May 1942, pp. 507-511.

Index

G

H

T

U

V

W